The Making of the Minister

Published by
Wildfire Publishing House
Manufactured in the UK
www.wildfirepublishinghouse.com

The Making of the Minister

Love Judah Ashiegbu

The Making of the Minister

Copyright © 2012 by
Love Judah Ashiegbu

ISBN 978-978-923-375-5

All rights reserved. No part of this publication may be reproduced, distributed, or transmitted in any form or by any means, or stored in a database or retrieval system, without written permission.

Published by:

Wildfire
Publishing House

The Wildfire Publishing House publishes prestigious premium-class books you can be proud of.
For information please visit:
www.wildfirepublishinghouse.com

Printed in the United Kingdom.

To my Pastor, Rev. W.D. Favour, all my pastors, spiritual sons, and ministers of the gospel around the world.

Acknowledgements

How can a man achieve mighty results without God using great men and women like my parents, Evang. and Mrs Livinus & Ezioma Ashiegbu, my pastor, Rev. W.D. Favour, my wife Shalom, and my lovely children, Trust, Bishop, Love, and Worship.

Particularly, I appreciate Mrs. J. Osueke and Pastor Jessica Dulcie for their sacrifices.

God's grace.

Contents

Acknowledgements viii

Contents ix

Foreword xi

My Prayer xii

Introduction xiii

Soul Winning 14

Leadership Levels 19

7 Preaching Qualities 23

Stewardship 32

Territorial Conquest 41

The Place of Planning in Ministry 50

Ministry and Finance 55

The Making of a Pastor 66

Jethro's Principles 83

Power to Minister 87

Index 91

About the Author 94

Foreword

When an unprepared and untrained man takes the stage to lead others, the outcome is disastrous. Many lives and destinies have been maimed by the activities of individuals who assumed positions of spiritual authority and leadership without adequate training. This is definitely one of the problems facing today's so-called New Generation Churches.

Men and women are God's methods. Whenever God wants to make a vital difference in the lives of individuals, families, and nations, He sends a man or a woman. However, that man or woman must be passed through the crucible of divine preparation and discipline. This takes time – lots of time; but it is essential to the making of any leader.

This book particularly addresses those men and women aspiring to the noble office of a Pastor. In this case, the need for adequate preparation and thorough training is even more important. The author presents vital principles of spiritual leadership that are relevant to the spiritual and personal development of various aspects of the life of any would-be pastor.

There are no easy pathways to pastoral training and development; this book makes that point quite clear. However, it also encourages you to embrace the challenges associated with the making of a pastor. You will find this book easy to read. You will find it uplifting and inspiring. Most importantly, you will enjoy its rich biblical references on various aspects of Christian leadership.

I have had the privilege of knowing the author from the very first moments of his life. It has also been my honor to have been a part of his spiritual journey in more ways than a page can permit. I certainly recommend this book as a helpful training manual for all aspiring pastors and Christian leaders.

Rev. Wildfire D'Favour
Founding Pastor, Citizens Family
Author of *Can God Be Lonely?*

My Prayer

May you reach your desired spiritual and ministerial goals.

May you not stop where others stopped; but where God wants you to.

May heaven grant you the grace to avoid, conquer, and have constant victory over all ministerial pitfalls and satanic traps.

May God grant you all the wisdom needed to apply His divine principles.

May you become the best minister you can be.

May God make you a role model, an example, a pace-setter, a trail-blazer, and a mentor to many coming behind you.

May you never miss heaven after all your efforts, achievements and impact in Jesus' name. Amen.

Introduction

A family was so blessed with the gift of a son that they imagined what the future would be like for him. Being hopeful, seeing that the child was lovely and good looking, they gave him several names reflecting their conviction that he would definitely be of great use to his generation.

Unfortunately, few years later, disaster struck and this child of hope was inflicted with a deadly disease which changed certain things about him, including his smartness and some outstanding virtues that had initially impressed his parents. His hair turned white, his friends at school called him names that made him feel useless, especially to a world he was to face.

As he grew up, he didn't look anything like the star his parents always believed he would become.
"How can I make it?" became his regular question and worry.
"I am a fool", "I have nothing to offer", "I'm stupid", were among all the negative thoughts that tortured his soul.

Then, he met a man he had known all the years of his life and looked up to. This mentor spoke words into his world; words that battled with the negatives he had known, and made him believe he was still the best, rather than being just useful.

But, how could this be? This young lad became one of the young influences in ministry, and now shares most of the greatest secrets of life that changed his world, destiny, experiences and most importantly his God given ministry.

Sit down and have a feel of God's divine transforming words for your destiny. Because if God could do it for me, I am sure you will definitely become better and perfect.

I love you

Pastor Love Judah Ashiegbu

Chapter 1

Soul Winning

Evangelism is the art of communicating God's love for humanity, and a persuasion to accept and respond to this love. It is reconciling people to their loving Father in heaven through the sacrifice of His Son, our Lord and Saviour Jesus Christ, who died that the world should be saved through him. It is the Father's desire that all people may come to know and love Him with the totality of their being.

Simply put, evangelism is introducing a man to his Creator. Evangelism is the love from God flowing out of our lives to others. Everyone loves something; the point of evangelism therefore, is to redirect this love towards God through faith in Jesus Christ.

Soul winning flows out of a life lived in obedience to God's will. The key to making witnessing natural is simply praying for God's will to work through us. When we are yielded, evangelism becomes natural in our lives because of the indwelling of the Holy Spirit.

Your openness makes you accessible to people and they willingly want to be identified with you naturally. This special quality of openness comes only from God.

Philippians 2:13- *For it is God which worketh in you both to will and to do of his good pleasure.*

6 Facts About Soulwinning

There are six facts one must know about soul winning:

1. Soul winning is a true expression of wisdom.

The fruit of the righteous is a tree of life; and he that winneth souls is wise.[1]

It takes wisdom to be a soul winner because in soul winning, you deal with all aspects of an individual that are in opposition to the Word of God.

2. Soul winning is a guarantee for eternal honour and glory

Heaven is a place of hierarchy and your position is largely determined by the number of souls you turned to righteousness. So many individuals have not yet come to the realization that their part in eternity is determined by the steps they take here on earth.

The wise shall inherit glory, but shame shall be the promotion of fools.[2]

'And many of them that sleep in the dust of the earth shall awake, some to everlasting life and some to shame and everlasting contempt. And they that be wise shall shine as the brightness of the firmament; and they that turn many to righteousness as the stars forever and ever.'[3]

3. There is a curse on any believer that does not win souls or preach the gospel.

Many ministers do not have the understanding that there are unusual blessings attached to soul winning, so much that heaven is definitely involved in favour of soul winners. In the same light, curses await anyone who happens to be part of Christendom, but is not actively involved in soul winning.

'For though I'll preach the gospel, I have nothing to glory of, for the necessity is laid upon me, yea, woe is unto me, if I preach not the Gospel. For if I do this thing willingly, I have a reward, but if against my will, a

---

[1] Proverbs 11:30
[2] Proverbs 3:35.
[3] Daniel 12:2-3.

dispensation of the Gospel is committed unto me.'[4]

4. To be an effective soul winner, you must be 'all things to all men.'

Many abuse the Gospel by not being prepared to humble themselves before men for the sake of winning them to Christ.

'For though I am free from all men yet, I have made myself a servant unto all that I might gain more. And unto the Jew (Believers), I became as a Jew, that I gain the Jews; to them that are under the law, as under the law, that I might gain them that are under the law; to them that are without the law (unbelievers), as without law, (being not without law to God, but under the law to Christ,) that I might gain them that are without the law; To the weak became I as weak, that I might gain the weak; I am made all things to all men that I might by all means save some.'[5]

5. The key to soul winning is love

'For God so **loved** the world, that He gave His only begotten Son, that whosoever believeth in him should not perish, but have everlasting life For God sent not His Son into the world to condemn the world but that the world through him might be saved.'[6]

Condemnation and a judgmental spirit is not the best approach to soul winning.

Hatred stirreth up strife, but **love** covereth all sins.

Every sinner has the guilt of sin but **love** is the perfect agent for change.[7]

'Husbands, love your wives, even as Christ also loved the church and gave himself for it; That He might sanctify and cleanse it with the washing of water by the Word, That He might present it to himself, a glorious church not having spot or wrinkle, or any such thing; but that it

---

[4] 1 Corinthians 9:16-17.
[5] 1 Corinthians 9:19-22.
[6] John 3:16-17.
[7] Proverbs 10:12.

should be holy and without blemish.'⁸

There is one important thing that the Church owes the world and that alone is the love that reaches out without condemnation or rejection. Once this is in place, it becomes easier to win souls.

6. A soul winner does not only just save souls from hell but saves himself too.

Take heed unto thyself and unto the doctrine, continue in them; for in doing this thou shalt save both thyself and them that hear thee⁹.

The Word of God is a double-edged sword; it is a searchlight on who you preach to and also on yourself. As a channel of salvation, you are being cleansed thoroughly as you preach, and the consciousness of God begins to build in you.

It also enhances your ministerial performance. The more you teach, the more you improve on your teaching skills.

It is also important for one to be concerned about one's areas of vulnerability. This indicates that the soul winner must be conscious of his/her areas of weakness, so as not to be a victim to satanic traps. Every time you come in contact with a sinner, understand that you are also a target, and it is dangerous to be a prey in the hands of someone you want to convert.

3 Effective Methods of Soul Winning

There are three effective methods of soul winning. They are:

1. Sharing a Word of Truth

This is interesting and usually done in a less formal manner, it is sharing a brief portion of the Bible or Word of truth with an individual. It simply means saying what you can about the Lord Jesus Christ in a few words. God will begin to use you increasingly as you learn to share the word of truth anytime and everywhere he wants you to; and as you mature, less

---

⁸ Ephesians 5: 25-27.
⁹ 1 Timothy 4:16.

and less prompting will be needed to motivate you in the direction of His will.

2. Sharing Your Testimony

The second method of evangelism is sharing an effective personal testimony. That is telling the story of how you came to know Christ as Your Lord and Saviour. You can also give many different kinds of testimonies with appropriate scriptural verses built into your testimony. Also identify with people's weaknesses and needs as truthfully as you can; because a lot of people can still spot your falsehood, and God is never glorified by the sin of exaggeration.

3. Sharing God's plan of Salvation

Mere words can't adequately describe the price God paid to make forgiveness possible. To share God's plan of salvation is to show that sinless, victorious, living is possible. His very name explains His divine nature and mission, "Christ" alone, not religion, or good works. Christ stands out as man's single source of salvation.

"Neither is there salvation on any other, for there is no other name under heaven given among men whereby we must be saved".[10]

People everywhere are hungry for Jesus Christ and salvation, but many of them do not know what or how to satisfy their hunger; they are searching for God, but often times, they don't even know who or what they are looking for.

Sharing the word of truth enables you to find out a personal level of interest in spiritual things, while your testimony reveals the reality of Christ in your experience. The plan of salvation indicates the simplicity involved in receiving the gift of forgiveness and eternal life.

---

[10] Acts 4:12.

Chapter 2

Leadership Levels

In a successful ministerial setting, the minister of the Gospel ought to consciously know and ascertain his level of impact per time and considerably make efforts to upgrade it.

There are five main levels in leadership and they are as follows:

a) Position.

b) Permission.

c) Production.

d) Reproduction.

e) Personhood.

Position

This is the stage where people follow you because they have to follow you.

They follow you at this level, simply because they are mandated by a higher authority to do so. What you have at this level is merely a title, since you were made a leader over them. When you are operating at this level you can't achieve much. There might be high turnover but it is rarely sustainable.

Permission

This is the level where people follow you because they want to follow you.

This level is achieved by relationship, care, and love. At this level people simply respond to you based on your attitude towards them. If you settle for this level, there is the danger of familiarity. As a Pastor, it is part of your responsibility to guard against becoming familiar with your people. It is very unhealthy in ministry and it also brings contempt. The wise or dynamic minister will transcend this level, while the wise and dynamic follower will get bored and search for something more.

Production

At this level of production people follow you because you achieve results or you are an achiever.

Here the leader is goal-oriented. People like associating with achievers much more than the regular ministers; it also breeds respect because they are encouraged by the leader's dynamism and innovation. This is the level where the minister's success is seen by people, and they like you and what you are doing. The world is hungry for people who will motivate and inspire them to succeed. It is very natural for people to drift towards you when you are successful.

This level gives you the opportunity to break into higher ministerial limelight.

Reproduction

This is the level where people follow you because of what you have done for them.

And this is the reason why you must transcend the level of production.

Hence, you must train people to become achievers like you are, by influencing their lives positively.

Your greatest burden as a leader should be to reproduce yourself. It is a pointer to how successful you've become. As they say, you are not a success until you have a successor. As a matter of fact, you are not a successful leader when you are not a role model to the people you are leading. People should desire to be like you, dress like you, talk like you, act or behave like you, and so on. This is how long lasting- growth and success in leadership are achieved. Reproduction of leaders ensures ongoing growth in an organization.

To maintain this level you have to do the following:

1. *You must constantly maintain relevance and improve in whatever you are doing, that makes them see you as a leader.*

If thou put the brethren in remembrance of these things, thou shalt be a good minister of Jesus Christ, nourished up *in* the words of faith and of good doctrine, whereunto thou has attained.[1]

Wherefore I put thee in remembrance that thou stir up the gift of God, which is in thee by the putting of my hands.[2]

Refresh your ideas, keep upgrading yourself: A great leader should not run out of ideas. Rather, improve on your ministerial skills.

Study to shew thyself approved unto God, a workman that needeth not to be ashamed, rightly dividing the word of truth.[3]

2. *Build discipline and character.*

These two factors are the major areas where *ministers* crash!

Your gift will take you up but character will either sustain you or bring you down. Here, you develop principles that will guide your life. You have to be very conscious about what you do in life and in your relationships with people. If you maintain this level in leadership, definitely you will get to the last level- personhood.

---

[1] 1 Timothy 4:6.
[2] 2 Timothy 1:6.
[3] 2 Timothy 2:15.

Personhood

And I will make thee a great nation, and I will bless thee, and make thy name great; and thou shalt be a blessing.[4]

At the four previous levels, people follow who you are and what you represent; but at the level of personhood, your name and person are greater than the ministry; and only few attain this height in leadership.

Finally, you can't skip levels; it has to be from stage to stage because leadership generally is a process.

---

[4] Genesis 12:2.

Chapter 3

7 Preaching Qualities

"**H**ow then shall they call on him on whom they have not believed? And how shall they believe in him of whom they have not heard? And how shall they hear without a preacher? And how can they preach except they be sent? As it is written, how beautiful are the feet of them that preach the gospel of peace, and bring glad tidings of good things! But they have not all obeyed the gospel. For Esaias saith, Lord, who hath believed our report? So then, faith cometh by hearing, and hearing by the Word of God.1

If you want souls to be saved, you must give maximum attention to preaching the gospel. Souls are saved by preaching. It is only on rare occasions that God appears to convert a soul.

Our ordination into ministry or priesthood is to preach. We have been counted worthy to be ambassadors of Christ.

"For this is good and acceptable in the sight of God our Saviour; who will have all men to be saved, and to come unto the knowledge of the truth. For there is One God, and one Mediator between God and men, the man Christ Jesus,[6] who gave Himself a ransom for all, to be testified in due time. Whereunto I am ordained a preacher and an apostle, (I speak the truth in Christ, and lie not); a teacher of the Gentiles in faith and verity".[2]

If you must not disappoint God in the ministry, you must consciously work toward getting all the qualities that will make the delivery of your

---

[1] Romans 10:14-17.
[2] 1 Timothy 2:3-7.

message effective. These qualities are as follows:

Physical Fitness

'Wilt thou shew wonders to the dead? Shall the dead praise thee?'[3]

'For the living know that they shall die, but the dead know not anything, neither have they any more reward, for the memory of them is forgotten. Also their love, and their hatred, and their envy, is now perished; neither have they any more a portion forever in anything that is under the sun.'[4]

Let us establish an important fact first, which is, that you need to be alive to preach; no dead man can preach the Gospel, much more having preaching qualities. A healthy body embodies a healthy spirit. Without a healthy body you cannot be effective in ministry.

You need to be sound to make others sound. You must attend to proper healthy living. Your physical health is very important and to keep it intact, there are three aspects you must give attention:

1. Dieting

Eat properly. One must know how his body functions so as not to put the body in a sub-optimal state, especially when you have to minister.

Drink no longer water, but use a little wine for thy stomach's sake and thine own infirmities.[5]

2. Exercise

Physical exercise is quite helpful.

For bodily exercise profiteth little, but godliness is profitable unto all things, having promise of the life of that which is yet to come.[6]

3. Rest

---

[3] Psalm 88:10.
[4] Ecclesiastes 9:5-6.
[5] 1 Timothy 5:23.
[6] 1 Timothy 4:8.

Let us consider how God responds to this issue of rest:

Be ye therefore followers of God as dear children.[7]

And on the seventh day God ended his work which he had made, and he rested on the seventh day from all his work which he had made.[8]

To everything there is a season, and a time to every purpose under heaven.[9]

According to God's divine order, there is a time to work and the time to rest.

One of my father's favourite rhetoric is 'You can't finish the work of God alone. When you die, this gospel will continue and God will keep raising men and women from across the world to continue from where both you and others stopped'. And I agree with him.

Come unto me, all ye that labour and are heavy laden and I will give you rest. Take my yoke upon you and learn of me, for I am meek and lowly in heart and ye shall find rest unto your souls. For my yoke is easy, and my burden is light.[10]

Jesus promises every minister rest; not just the bodily one but also the rest of the soul. Many ministers of the Gospel do not have rest in their minds and this is very challenging, because if the mind is not at rest, it will definitely affect the work and performance of the minister.

Boldness

Son of man, I have made thee a watchman unto the house of Israel. Therefore hear the word at my mouth and give them warning from me. When I say unto the wicked, thou shalt surely die, and thou givest him not warning, speakest to warn the wicked from his wicked way to save his life; the same wicked man shall die in his iniquity but his blood will I

---

[7] Ephesians 5:1.
[8] Genesis 2:2.
[9] Ecclesiastes 3:1.
[10] Matt 11:28-30.

require at thine hand.[11]

Always, there are forces focused on you each time you stand on the sacred desk as well as whenever the Lord places or lays a strong mandate in your heart. These forces are there to make sure you are not effective. These forces could be spiritual, psychological, emotional or social; and at such times *boldness* is needed for effective performance and delivery.

To operate in boldness, you must know that it is different from self confidence. The difference between the two is that boldness is a product of divine contact with the Spirit of Jesus. It helps you to withstand these satanic oppositions and forces, whenever you are confronted with them.

Now when they saw the boldness of Peter and John and perceived that they were unlearned and ignorant men, they marvelled; and they took knowledge of them, that they had been with Jesus.[12]

And when they had prayed, the place was shaken where they were assembled together, and they were filled with the Holy Ghost; and they spake the Word of God with boldness.[13]

Imagination

Every good preacher must learn to use his sense of imagination that is, have the ability to create pictures in the mind while ministering, using parables and illustrations to buttress points.

The ministry of Jesus was characterized by the use of parables, illustrations and most of all, the power of imagination.

And the disciples came and said unto him, why speakest thou unto them in parables? He answered and said unto them, because it was given unto you the mysteries of the kingdom of heaven but to them it is not given.[14]

All these things spake Jesus unto the multitude in parables, and without

---
[11] Ezekiel 3:17-18.
[12] Acts 4:13.
[13] Acts 4:31.
[14] Matt. 13:10-11.

a parable spake he not unto them. That it might be fulfilled which was spoken by the prophets saying, I will open my mouth in parables, I will utter things which have been kept secret from the foundation of the world.[15]

Maturity in ministry is also seen in your ability to create mental pictures instantly to further elaborate on a point.

Be a student of nature and events around you because there are lectures in nature. This implies that, your mind must be involved if you want to be an effective preacher.

Gracious Speech

Let your speech be always with grace, seasoned with salt, that ye might know how ye ought to answer every man[16]

How beautiful upon the mountains are the feet of him that bringeth good tidings, that publisheth peace, that bringeth good tidings of good, that publisheth salvation; that saith unto Zion, thy God reigneth![17]

What kind of news do you utter from the sacred desk?

Learn to be gracious with words and not judgmental.

The preparations of the heart is in the man, and the answer of the tongue is from the LORD.[18]

Circumcise your heart to always feed your tongue with gracious words by building a strong level of intimacy with God.

There is that speaketh like the piercings of a sword, but the tongue of the wise is health. The lips of truth shall be established forever, but a lying tongue is but for a moment.[19]

A soft answer turneth away wrath, but grievous words stir up anger.

---

[15] Matt 13:34-35.
[16] Colossians 4:6
[17] Isaiah 52:7
[18] Proverbs 16:1
[19] Proverbs 12:18-19.

The tongue of the wise useth knowledge aright, but the mouth of fools poureth out foolishness.[20]

No corrupt word should proceed out of your mouth especially when you are on the pulpit.

Two Areas to work on:

1. Vocabulary

It is so needful to understand the level and class of people you minister to; this goes a long way to determine your choice of words and vocabulary. This is essential, as you can quite easily lose your audience to grammatical errors.

And Solomon told her all her questions; there was not anything hid from the king which he told her not. And when the queen of Sheba had seen all Solomon's wisdom and the house that he had built And the meat of his table, and the sitting of his servants, and the attendance of his ministers, and their apparel, and his cupbearers, and his ascent by which he went up unto the house of the LORD, there was no more spirit in her.[21]

2. Speaking Style

Choose a speaking style that will help you communicate easily without being misunderstood.

The wise in heart shall be called prudent; and the sweetness of the lips increaseth learning.[22]

Possessing A Sweet Personality

A sweet personality is the uniqueness you have that others don't have. It attracts people to you. To be an effective preacher, you must discover this uniqueness. A sweet personality is part of the godly nature in you and everybody has it. You should develop grace and a sweet personality as a minister.

---

[20] Proverbs 15:1
[21] 1 Kings 10:3-5.
[22] Proverbs 16:21.

Now these be the last words of David, David the son of Jesse said, and the man who was raised up on high, the anointed of the God of Jacob, and the sweet psalmist of Israel, said, "The Spirit of the Lord spake by me and his word was in my mouth."[23]

How To Develop A Sweet Personality

1. Desire

You must desire it and have a role model or a father with a pleasing personality/charisma who inspires or mentors you. You cannot desire what you have not seen. If you have a sweet personality/charisma, you will command crowds.

2. Prayer

You can also pray for a sweet personality. When the glory of God overshadows you, everyone will like to be identified with you. The anointing is so attractive and not so many ministers have it. Prayer is basically spending time with God, and once you meet God, men would want to meet you.

3. Develop Your Gifts

First discover your gift and develop it. Wise people emphasize their areas of strength while fools emphasize their areas of weakness.

A Charismatic Personality can be seen in these three areas:

Sensitivity to the Spirit

This is one of the core requirements for a Pastor. Once you have it, people will want to be identified with you. Sensitivity could be to know when the Spirit of God is present and what the Spirit is saying per time.

Enthusiasm

Enthusiasm means a strong excitement, passion, zeal or strong feeling

---
[23] 2 Samuel 23:1-2.

for a cause. It also means to be imaginative and to have freedom from fear or doubt especially when it has to do with what you are doing. It also means having an inner power and always in control of your senses. A man that must rule the world, must rule himself (his spirit) first.

You have to electrify your listeners with enthusiasm. Enthusiasm for a cause is contagious and infectious. It comes from within and is magnetic.

Blessed is the people that know the joyful sound; they shall walk, O Lord in the light of thy countenance. In thy name shall they rejoice all the day, and in thy righteousness they be exalted.[24]

Sensitivity to People's Needs

Being sensitive to people's needs involves feeling their pains, sharing their joy and difficult moments and above all, interceding for them in prayers. You have to be a comfort to the broken hearted as a Pastor/Minister.

You must learn to comfort and make people happy. All these should be seen in your preaching or ministrations. Be a problem solver and do all in love as you cannot meet people's needs without loving them.

Physical Appearance and Dressing

You are addressed the way you dress. Your dressing speaks a lot about you. As a Pastor/Minister, people will always assess you first by your outward appearance. A minister's attire should be glorious, and our dressing must represent God and His kingdom.

As a minister, there are two basic reasons why you dress: glory and beauty.

And thou shalt make holy garments for Aaron thy brother, for glory and for beauty. And thou shalt speak unto all that are wise hearted, whom I have filled with the Spirit of wisdom, that they make Aaron's garment to consecrate him, that he may minister unto me in the priest's office.[25]

---

[24] Psalm 89:15-16.
[25] Exodus 28:2-3.

Hard Work

The hand of the diligent shall bear rule, but the slothful shall be under tribute.[26]

Be thou diligent to know the state of thy flocks, and look well to thy herds. For riches are not forever, and doth the crown endure to every generation? The hay appeareth, and the tender grass sheweth itself and herbs of the mountain are gathered. The lambs are for thy clothing and the goats are the price of the field. And thou shalt have goats' milk enough for thy food, for the food of thy household, and for the maintenance for thy maidens.[27]

Success in ministry responds to hard work. This means that there are critical aspects you must give diligence to:

4 Aspects of Hard Work

1. Diligence in knowing the state of your flock.

2. Diligence in studying the scriptures.

If you want to do well and preach well, then study the scriptures. This is the most important aspect you must attend to.

3. Diligence in planning your message.

Put down your ideas on paper, organize your speech and message before presentation.

4. Diligence in counselling and visitation.

Part of your work is visitation, and the more you talk to people, the more influential you become. People always gravitate towards men who sincerely care about whatever they need. However, this must be done with utmost caution and frugality before people take your visits for granted and familiarity sets in.

---

[26] Proverbs 12:24.
[27] Proverbs 27:23-27.

Chapter 4

Stewardship

To have a perfect understanding of stewardship in its totality, proper and detailed analysis must be made especially for clarity, in order to avoid ambiguity.

Stewardship has to do with a master-servant relationship. Being a servant or disciple is the same thing. As a leader you must discover who your true disciples or servants are. Ministries crumble and churches close down because the master is not sure of whom his true stewards are.

You have to be sure of the people that run your church system. Are they faithful or deceitful stewards?

You also need to discern the people around you to know and ascertain if they are faithful or not.

Yea, mine own familiar friend, in whom I trusted, which did eat my bread

hath lifted his heel against me.[1]

Basic Guides on Master-Steward Relationship

And straightway he constrained his disciples to get into the ship and to go to the other side before unto Bethsaida, while he sent away the

---

[1] Psalm 41:9.

people.[2]

Jesus forced his disciples to be separated from the multitude and get into a ship.

a. A master gives his disciples instructions and gives the multitude suggestions.

b. A master commands the disciples while he appeals to the multitude.

c. The 'ship' represents 'relationship', you get into a relationship with disciples, not the multitudes. If anybody needs to know you or your secrets, it is your disciples. Intimate relationship should be with the disciples and not the multitude. You should also know what to share with people because it is your inner people that will betray your secrets.

d. You can rely on your disciples and release the multitude. It is easier to discover who your master is and rely on him than finding a true steward you can rely on.

12 Things You Need to Know About A Faithful Steward

The key word for stewardship is faithfulness. The number "12" represents discipleship, so there are 12 things you need to know about a faithful steward.

Suffice to say that, there are a lot of Bible heroes, so we need a thorough search into the scriptures to discover men with unique, amazing and godly qualities, whose lives and principles if carefully studied and put into practice can change a whole lot of things in ministry and Christendom at large. One of such men is Eliezer, Abraham's steward.

So let's pick out 12 points from his life and principles:

---

[2] Mark 6:45.

1. A faithful steward must have a specific mission[3].

As a good steward, you cannot succeed without a good understanding of the mission. You must understand:

   a. The sender

   b. The message and

   c. The audience/people

You must take time to understand the vision or mission that God or His servants want you to embark on.

2. A faithful steward must have all his master's goods at his disposal[4].

To represent your master, you must have all his 'goods' to function adequately. These goods could be ability, gifts, power or anointing, knowledge and understanding. It could also be riches, wealth or connections. The possession of these goods will go a long way to determine how successful you will become as a steward, especially when you are on a mission.

3. A faithful steward must be a man of prayer[5].

The greatest secret to taking over a land or nation is prayers. You cannot succeed in a vision without prayer because you can't take away a strong man's city without first binding him.

Or else how can one enter into a strong man's house and spoil his goods, except he first bind the strong man? And then he will spoil his house.[6]

Prayer was the key secret of Jesus in ministry. When you fail to pray, you remain a prey.

---

[3] Genesis 24:1-9.
[4] Genesis 24:10.
[5] Genesis 24:1-14.
[6] Matthew 12:29-.

4. A good steward worships God for his breakthroughs, successes, favour, miracles and does not boast about them.[7]

A faithful steward does not see man as the key to his breakthroughs but sees God because once your link with God is intact, the flow will remain. A good steward will remember and acknowledge that God is his source and giver of every good he has, even his life. What God does is that he uses men as channels of his blessings. With God in your labours, you cannot be stranded, frustrated or lack testimonies and results.

5. A good steward is preceded with favour, goodwill and glorious reception and acceptance.[8]

God goes ahead of a faithful steward to prepare a place for him. To get favour and acceptance, a steward must apply his master's goods.

He is equipped and prepared with the first four points, to the extent that anybody who encounters the good steward will delight to keep him for life. God goes before you; hence you don't struggle to achieve results. A good steward is equipped in all things.

Not that I speak in respect of want, for I have learned in whatsoever state I am, therewith to be content. I know both how to be abused, and I know how to abound; everywhere and in all things I am instructed both to be full and to be hungry, both to abound and to suffer need. I can do all things through Christ which strengtheneth me.[9]

6. A faithful steward has self control in a foreign land[10]

Mission must come first before pleasure. The four areas a minister needs self control are

---

[7] Genesis 24:26-27.
[8] Genesis 24:28-31.
[9] Philipians 4:11-13.
[10] Genesis 24:33.

(a) Food

When thou sittest to eat with a ruler, consider diligently what is set before thee. And put a knife to thy throat, if thou be a man given to appetite. Be not desirous of his dainties; for they are deceitful meat[11].

The first discipline needed is in the area of food. You should remember that man shall not live by bread alone; (Matt. 4:4), don't eat away your anointing, destiny and future.

Hear thou, my son and be wise, and guide thine heart in the way, Be not among wine bibbers, among riotous eaters of flesh; For the drunkard and the glutton shall come to poverty. And drowsiness shall clothe a man in rags.[12]

(b) Immoral relationships or immorality

If you don't control it, it will cripple you. Many great leaders, rulers and ministers have come to ruins, all because of the inability to control their sexual desires.

See Proverbs 7:5-27

Flee also youthful lusts; but follow righteousness, faith, charity, peace with them that call on the Lord out a pure heart.[13]

(c) Money

A lot of ministers derail because of the pursuit of money. Don't eat your destiny; Esau sold his birthright out of a desire for cheap momentary pleasure.

Woe unto them! For they have gone in the way of Cain, and ran greedily after the error of Balaam for reward, and perished in the gainsaying of Korah. These are spots in your feasts of charity, when they feast with you, feeding themselves without fear, clouds they are without water, carried about of winds, trees whose fruit wherewith, without fruit, twice

---

[11] Proverbs 23:1-3.
[12] Proverbs 23:19-21.
[13] 2 Timothy 2:22.

dead, plucked up by the roots.[14]

Let us not be gain-conscious, money is a tool to help you achieve your vision or mission. Don't allow anyone control you with money. Where you are going to is too great to be compared with where you are now; so don't jeopardise your future.

But godliness with contentment is great gain. For we brought nothing into this world, and it is certain we can carry nothing out. And having food and raiment, let us be therewith content. But they that will be rich fall into temptation and a snare and into many foolish and hurtful lusts, which drown men in destruction and perdition. For the love of money is the root of all evil, which while some coveted after, they have erred from the faith, and pierced themselves through with many sorrows. But thou, O man of God, flee these things and follow after righteousness, godliness, faith, love, patience, meekness.[15]

(d) Self control in words

If any man among you seem to be religious and bridleth not his tongue, but decieveth his own, this man's religion is vain[16].

A good steward should have self-control in words. He should be conscious of when to talk and when not to talk. Words can either build or destroy.

See James 3:1-13

There are times when you swallow your words. It is not everything you see that you say. Delay gratification until your mission is accomplished, and the mission must come before pleasure.

7. A faithful steward has the virtue of humility[17]

He must know that he is a servant, and he must always be humble in carrying out his master's assignment.

---

[14] Jude 11-12.
[15] 1 Timothy 6:6-11.
[16] James 1:26-
[17] Genesis 24:34.

Servants be obedient to them that are your masters according to the flesh, with fear and trembling, in singleness of your heart, as unto Christ;

Not with eye service, as men-pleasers, but as servants of Christ, doing the will of God from the heart.[18]

The greatest enemies of humility are pride and ego; and to address them, the following steps are necessary:

(a) Consider others better than yourself.

Be kindly affectionate one to another with brotherly love in honour, preferring one another.[19]

(b) Be not wise in your own eyes

Be of the same mind toward another. Mind not high things, but condescend to men of low estate. Be not wise in your own conceit.[20]

(c) Continuously be aware of your weaknesses

Therefore I take pleasure in infirmities, in reproaches, in necessities, in persecutions, in distresses for Christ's sake; for when I am weak, then I am strong.[21]

Know your faults so as not to be judgmental; true lifting in stewardship is a product of humility. The first and greatest sin is pride.

The greatest keys to humility are:

- Making oneself of no reputation, and giving up some privileges.
- Taking the form of a servant or slave.

Humility must be considered to be one's sole responsibility and is achieved through the help of God and the conscious decision of the person.

---

[18] Ephesians 6:5-6.
[19] Romans 12:10-.
[20] Romans 12:16-
[21] 2 Corinthians 12:10.

Let this mind be in you which was also in Christ Jesus. Who being in the form of God thought it not robbery to be equal with God. But made himself of no reputation, and took upon him the form of a servant, and was made in the likeness of men. And being found in fashion as a man, he humbled himself and became obedient unto death, even the death of the cross.[22]

Humility is not being foolish, possessing an inferior feeling, or just being stupid. It does not show in one part and not in another, but it shows in all things and in all areas of your life.

8. A faithful steward gives a true and faithful description of his master[23]

Every leadership must face criticisms but a faithful steward protects the integrity of his master. A faithful description of your master should include:

a. Giving credit to your master for playing a significant role in your life.

b. Proper representation: Most times stewards are not proud of their leaders, and this affects how leaders are being addressed and represented.

Be not thou therefore ashamed of the testimony of our Lord, nor of me His prisoner; but be thou partaker of the gospel according to the power of God.[24]

9. A faithful steward is zealous, has integrity and a sense of mission[25]

10. A faithful steward is not selfish but seeks the good of the kingdom, his master and that of others[26]

---

[22] Philippians 2:5-8.
[23] Genesis 24:35.
[24] 2 Timothy 1:8-.
[25] Genesis 24:54-56.
[26] Genesis 24:53.

A faithful steward is not selfish but shows genuine concern for others. **(Genesis 24:53)**

11. A faithful steward is submissive to hierarchy[27]

Without a submissive heart, one cannot go far in leadership. You must submit to everyone higher than you in leadership.

12. A faithful steward has a sense of accountability[28]

It includes being accountable for every duty, giving a detailed report of your duties. Also, proper explanation should be made to your leadership when required.

When we talk of stewardship, our stewardship goes to:

a. God

b. Our Mentor and

c. The Vision

In summary, this study can be called Eleazer's principles, because he was very outstanding particularly in the aspect of stewardship.

Furthermore these principles, if carefully studied and practiced, guarantee the development of a proper leadership capacity.

---

[27] Genesis 24:64-65.
[28] Genesis 24:66.

Chapter 5

Territorial Conquest

To be successful as a pastor, a minister must know that he is not just dealing with humans but also spiritual territories.

A minister should have the capacity to conquer any territory no matter how hard or tough.

Now the LORD had said unto Abram, get thee out of thy country, and from thy kindred, and from thy father's house, unto a land that I will shew thee. And I will make thee a great nation, and I will bless thee, and make thy name great, and thou shalt be a blessing And I will bless them that bless thee; and curse him that curseth thee; and in thee shall all families of the earth be blessed.[1]

Abraham was the first person in the bible that conquered territories. He understood the capacity God deposited in him, by that mandate (going anywhere and taking over); that was why he told his nephew Lot to choose where he would abide, because he knew within himself that with the capacity he had, he would succeed anywhere! He knew what he was carrying.

His nephew Lot choose the portion of land to abide, on the basis of its apparent fertility.

Ministry is not about where you know people or where you have strong ties and connections.

---
[1] Genesis 12:1-3

Abraham understood that anywhere he went, he would succeed.

Secrets of Territorial Invasion

1. Understanding the Mandate

Many ministers fail because they don't have a perfect understanding of what God wants them to do. In some cases, some don't even have a mandate and this can be very disastrous.

2. Having the mind of Christ

The product of a renewed mind is phenomenal results. I am an heir of Abraham's promises and blessings[2] and because I have that same grace, I will not fail in anything or place. I must learn to defeat the devil in my thinking first to be able to capture a territory. Abraham's grace still continued in Isaac and Jacob. Jacob's successes in Laban's house is traceable to the mandate of Abraham. Anywhere you are placed, you should be able to gather the ants if you have the grace.

For wherever the carcass is, there will the eagles gather.[3]

No matter where you are, if there is the manifestation of these two secrets, people will gather. It is not about the site, but the mind. It is about the capacity of the person there. Your thoughts direct your actions, so think big and positive.

In addition, there are unique keys which if applied produces phenomenal results in ministry.

Keys to Territorial Invasion

1. Love and Affection

Love is not a feeling. To love means to choose a set of actions based on the word of God with respect to your dealings with other people. You don't love because you feel like loving, you rather develop an

---
[2] Galatians 3:14,29
[3] Matthew 24:28

attitude based on the word of God towards everyone, so that all can feel accommodated and loved. With this attitude in a strange land, you can love everyone without restraint.

But it displeased Jonah exceedingly, and he was very angry. And he prayed unto the LORD, and said, I pray thee, O LORD, was not this my saying when I was yet in my country? Therefore I fled before unto Tarshish; for I knew that thou art a gracious God, and merciful, slow to anger and of great kindness, and repentest thee of evil. Therefore now O LORD, take I beseech thee, my life from me, for it is better for me to die than to live. Then saith the LORD, doest thou well to be angry?[4]

In ministry, except you stick out your neck you can't work or walk with people. This is because as you relate with people, you must find deficiencies, but you must learn to overlook them and continue your work with them. It takes the strength of your relationship with God to love people. The closer you are to God, the easier it is to love people because God is love.

For this saith the Lord God, Behold I, even I will both search my sheep and seek them out. As a shepherd seeketh out his flock on the day that he is among his sheep that are scattered, so will I seek out my sheep, and will deliver them out of all places where they have been scattered in the cloudy and dark day. And I will bring them out from the people, and gather them from the countries, and will bring them to their own land, and feed them upon the mountains of Israel by the rivers and in all the inhabited places of the country. I will feed them in a good pasture and upon the high mountains of Israel shall their fold be; there shall they lie in a good fold and in a fat pasture shall they feed upon the mountains of Israel. I will feed my flock, and I will cause them to lie down saith the Lord GOD. I will seek that which was lost and bring again that which was driven away, and I will bind up that which was broken, and will strengthen that which was sick; but I will destroy the fat and the strong, I will feed them with judgment.[5]

By this you don't need to be in the centre of the church to rule the church, but as the need of the people becomes your need, people feel love and understand love through your actions.

---

[4] Jonah 4:1-4
[5] Ezekiel 34:11-16

2. Walking with God

The greatest mistake any pastor can make, is to work for God and not walk with Him. In territorial invasion, don't be interested in working for God until you have a personal relationship with Him.

Enoch walked with God after he begat Methuselah three hundred years, and begat sons and daughters. And all the days of Enoch were three hundred sixty and five years. And Enoch walked with God, and he was not, for God took him.[6]

Intimacy should precede activity. Spend more time with God than with people and agree with God in your heart and in your mind concerning any vision or assignment.

Therefore David inquired of the LORD saying, shall I go and smite these Philistines? And the LORD said unto David, Go, and smite the Philistines, and save Keilah. And David's men said unto him, behold we be afraid here in Judah, how much more if we come to Keilah against the armies of the Philistines? Then David inquired of the Lord yet again, and the Lord answered him adn said, Arise, go down to Keilah, for I will deliver the Philistines into thine hand.[7]

Don't do anything without a divine direction from God. Always find out what God is saying about your church and your flock. You will stay successful if you keep in step with God's instructions.

I am not able to bear all these people alone because it is too heavy for me. And if thou deal thus with me, kill me, I pray thee, out of hand, if I have found favour in thy sight, and let me not see my wretchedness. And the LORD said unto Moses, Gather unto me seventy elders of Israel to whom thou knowest to be the elders of the people, and officers over them; and bring them unto the tabernacle of the congregation, that they may stand there with thee. And I will come down and talk with thee there, and I will take of the Spirit which is upon thee, and will put it upon them, and they shall bear the burden of the people with thee, that thou not bear it not thyself alone.[8]

---

[6] Genesis 5:22-24
[7] 1 Samuel 23:2-4
[8] Numbers 11:14-17

In walking with God, search out God's mind for His people and flock because walking with God helps you in your relationship with people. In ministry, there are issues only God can address in your life and also in the life of the people He wants you to lead. As a minister, cultivate the habit of talking with God first, on an issue, before sharing with anybody or anyone else.

3. Submission

We must not only submit to God, but also to leadership authorities, because when you disobey any authority, you are disobeying God.

Let every soul be subject unto the higher powers. For there is no power but of God; the powers that be are ordained of God. Whosoever therefore resisteth the power resisteth the ordinance of God; and they that resist shall receive to themselves damnation. For rulers are not a terror to good works, but to the evil. Wilt thou then not be afraid of the power? Do that which is good, and thou shall have praise of the same. For he is a minister of God to thee for good. But if thou do that which is evil, be afraid for he beareth not the sword in vain; for he is a minister of God, a revenger to execute wrath upon him that doeth evil. Wherefore ye must needs be subject, not only for wrath, but also for conscience's sake. For this cause pay ye tribute also, for they are God's ministers, attending continually upon this very thing. Render therefore to all their duties, tribute to whom tribute is due; custom to whom custom, fear to whom fear, honour to whom honour.[9]

We must endure pain and hardship in life considering leadership in missions; a minister must learn to submit to the directions of the vision of the authority of the church.

Servants, be obedient to them that are your masters according to the flesh, with fear and trembling, in singleness of your heart as unto Christ;Not with eye service, as men pleasers, but as servant of Christ doing the will of God from the heart.With goodwill doing service, as to the Lord, and not to men. Knowing that whatsoever good thing any man doeth, the same shall he receive of the Lord, whether he be bond or free.[10]

---

[9] Romans 13:1-7
[10] Ephesians 6:5-8

Obey those who are placed over you, and let your life be an example to those who are under you.

- Let as many servants as are under the yoke count their own masters worthy of all honor, that the name of God and his doctrine be not blasphemed.[11]

Every master knows the heart of his servant, for example, Jesus knew Judas, Elijah knew Elisha, and so on. This explains that every true leader by the principle of submission should be able to discern a submissive follower from a non-submissive one.

4. Praise and Thanksgiving

Learn to praise God always and rejoice in His presence and always allow your people to praise and give Him thanks in every situation.

- In all things give thanks, for this is the will of God in Christ Jesus concerning you[12].

The land yields increase to those who learn to praise in all circumstances.

Let the people praise thee, O God, let all the people praise thee. O let the nations be glad and sing for joy, for thou shalt judge the people righteously, and govern the nations upon the earth. Let the people praise thee, O God; let all the people praise thee. Then shall the earth yield her increase, and God even our own God shall bless us.[7] God shall bless us and all the ends of the earth shall fear him.[13]

Teach your people to thank God, for any small blessing or gift that comes from God.

Rejoice in the Lord always, and again I say rejoice. Let your moderation be known unto all men. The Lord is at hand. Be careful for nothing, but in everything by prayer and supplication with thanksgiving let your requests be made known unto God. And the peace of God which passeth all understanding shall keep your hearts and minds through Christ

---

[11] 1 Timothy 6:1
[12] *1 Thessalonians 5:18*
[13] Psalm 67:3-7

Jesus. *Finally, brethren, whatsoever things are true, whatsoever things are honest, whatsoever things are just, whatsoever things are pure, whatsoever things are lovely, whatsoever things are of good report, if there be any virtue, and if there be any praise, think on these things.*[14]

5. Fasting and Praying

Then Jesus was led up of the Spirit into the wilderness to be tempted of the devil. And when he had fasted forty days and forty nights, he was afterward a hungered.[15]

Jesus did not start his ministry without fasting first. He did 40 days fasting before the wilderness scene.

But so much the more he went there a fame abroad of him, and great multitudes came together to hear, and to be healed by him of their infirmities. And he withdrew himself into the wilderness and prayed. And it came to pass on a certain day, as he was teaching, that there were Pharisees and doctors of the law sitting by, which were come out of every town of Galilee, and Judea, and Jerusalem, and the power of God was present to heal them.[16]

The ministry of Jesus was linked to prayers; He did wonders in the day and prayed at night.

His divinity did not negate the power of prayer and fasting; rather His actions highlighted the fact that divinity needs continuous supernatural sustenance to remain relevant.

To buttress this point further, it is note-worthy to observe that His disciples fasted fifty days before they started their ministry.

And when the day of Pentecost was fully come, they were all with one accord in one place.[17]

Day of "Pentecost fully come" explains the 50 days fast.

---

[14] Philippians 4:4-8
[15] Matthew 4:1-2
[16] Luke 5:15-17
[17] Acts 2:1

And ye shall count unto you from the morrow after the Sabbath, from the day that ye brought the sheaf of the wave offering, seven Sabbaths shall be complete. Even unto the morrow after the seventh Sabbath shall ye number fifty days, and ye shall offer a new meat offering unto the LORD.[18]

So it is expedient that prior to going on missions or planting a church in other cities or country, one must engage in prayer and fasting. Prayer and fasting then becomes a preparation for clearing the ground or equipping the minister for the mission ahead.

[15] But so much the more he went there a fame abroad of him, and great multitudes came together to hear, and to be healed by him of their infirmities.

[16] And he withdrew himself into the wilderness and prayed. [17] And it came to pass on a certain day, as he was teaching, that there were Pharisees and doctors of the law sitting by, which were come out of every town of Galilee, and Judea, and Jerusalem, and the power of God was present to heal them.[19]

The ministry of Jesus was linked to prayers that He could do wonders in the day and prayed in the night.

His divinity did not negate the power of prayer and fasting but rather emphasized that divinity needs more supernatural sustenance to remain relevant.

Also, His disciples fasted fifty days before they started their ministry.

And when the day of Pentecost was fully come, they were all with one accord in one place.[20]

Day of "Pentecost fully come" explains the 50-day fast.

[15] And ye shall count unto you from the morrow after the Sabbath, from the day that ye brought the sheaf of the wave offering, seven Sabbaths shall be complete. [16] Even unto the morrow after the seventh Sabbath

---

[18] Leviticus 23:15-16
[19] Luke 5:15-17
[20] Acts 2:1

shall ye number fifty days, and ye shall offer a new meat offering unto the LORD.[21]

So it is a pre-requisite that going on missions or planting a church in other cities or country, one must engage in prayer and fasting. Prayer and fasting then becomes a preparation for clearing the ground or equipping the minister for the mission ahead.

---

[21] Lev 23:15-16

Chapter 6

The Place of Planning in Ministry

Mediocrity is so prevalent in the body of Christ today, because the place of planning has been neglected. An anointed head is an anointed brain which is what we use for planning.

Thou preparest a table before me in the presence of mine enemies, thou anointest my head with oil, my cup runneth over.[1]

In ministry, God does a quarter part of the work, while we do three quarters. There is more to what you are expected to do than what God is expected to do; the bulk of the work is in our hands. This is one of the most important aspects of ministry where most ministers fail; at the place of planning. Increase is always the corresponding result of an anointed head. In whatever we do, as long as the head is anointed, it must prosper. If the works of our hands are not flourishing, then something is wrong with the head. Good planning guarantees success in ministry and guarantees speed.

We serve a God of preparation and planning; and if He plans, then we should learn to plan.

For I know the thoughts that I think towards you saith the LORD, thoughts of peace, and not evil, to give you an expected end.[2]

When we talk about planning there are three things we must understand:

---

[1] Psalm 23:5
[2] Jeremiah 29:11

(1) Planning is being like God

(2) God expects us to plan

(3) We must submit our plans to God by fasting and prayer.

The preparations of the heart in man, and the answer of the tongue, is from the LORD. All the ways of a man are clean in his own eyes but the Lord weigheth the spirits Commit thy works unto the LORD and thy thoughts shall be established.[3]

There is no substitute for inspired planning. In planning, there are different types; and the issue to be planned determines the type you use:

- **Personal Planning**: This is the planning you do alone without getting anyone else involved. This works perfectly in pursuing your God-given destiny.
- **Corporate planning**: This type of planning involves mainly the executives of the ministry, church or the co-leadership body.
- **General Planning**: Involves not just the executives, but also the entire membership of the body or church.

Components of A Sound Plan

A sound plan must contain a clear picture of the end

You must know exactly what you want to achieve at any given time. You must not confuse your means with your end. For example, the programs or events organized are not an end, but a means; and the means might change. Don't allow it to distract you from your end. So before you take any step, determine your end and means.

And we desire that every one of you do shew the same diligence to the full assurance of hope unto the end.[4]

---

[3] Proverbs 16:1-3
[4] Hebrew 6:11

It is your destination that determines your direction and with this in perspective, speed can be determined also. So having your end in perspective is always very important. You don't asses yourself with others; you assess yourself with your end. This is the mistake many people make in ministry. You are not in competition with anybody but with your destiny. With this understanding, you must have a clear detailed picture of your end.

A Sound Plan Must Outline All the Necessary Steps between the Beginning and the End

And he said unto me, it is done. I am Alpha and Omega, the beginning and the end. I will give unto him that is athirst of the fountain of the water of life freely.[5]

God knows the end from the beginning, nothing that happens takes him unawares. Becoming like Him indicates that we ought to know at least to an extent, every necessary step to be undertaken.

I am Alpha and Omega, the beginning and the end, the first and the last.[6]

You must foresee the significant steps, the possible pitfalls, and have the analytical breakdown of all the necessary steps to be undertaken. The objective of every good leader is to make sure that these steps will not in any way derail you from achieving the end.

A Sound Plan Must Contain the Total Cost of the Task to Be Undertaken

For which of you, intending to build a tower sitteth not down first, and counteth the cost, whether he have sufficient to finish it? Lest haply, after he hath laid the foundation, and is not able to finish it, all that behold it begin to mock him, Saying, this man began to build and was not able to finish.[7]

---

[5] Revelation 21:6
[6] Revelation 22:13
[7] Luke 14:28-30

In costing, you must make sure that provision is made in advance before undertaking any task. A lot of people are being mocked because they live a plan-less life. So to avoid mockery, you must plan. At this stage, planning relieves you of the anxiety of the future, and in ministry you do not need anxiety; you need to relax so as to be coordinated and on top of the job.

A Sound Plan must Contain the Division of Labour for Specific Individuals

This includes specific actions, assignments or responsibilities for specific individuals. At this level you can determine your human resources, know their individual abilities and capacities; so as to commit the right duties to the right person.

Moreover thou shalt provide out of all the people, able men, such as fear God, men of truth, hating covetousness; and place such over them, to be rulers of thousands and rulers of hundreds, rulers of fifties and rulers of tens. And let them judge the people at all seasons, and it shall be that every great matter they shall bring unto thee, but every small matter they shall judge; so shall it be easier for thyself, and they shall bear the burden with thee.[8]

And Moses said unto he children of Israel, see the LORD hath called by name Bezalel the son of Uri, the son of Hur, of the tribe of Judah; And he hath filled him with the Spirit of God, in wisdom, in understanding, in knowledge and in all manner of workmanship; And to devise the curious works, to work in gold, and in silver, and in brass, And in the cutting of stones, to set them, and in carving of wood to make any manner of cunning work. And he hath put his heart that he may teach, both he and Oholiab, the son of Ahisamach, of the tribe of Dan. Them hath he filled with wisdom of heart, to work all manner of work, of the engraver, and of the cunning workman, and of the embroiderer, in blue, and in purple, in scarlet and in fine linen, and of the weaver, even of them that do any work, and of those that devise cunning work.[9]

A mistake at this stage can cause leadership shipwreck.

---

[8] Exodus 18:21-22
[9] Exodus 35:30-35

A Sound Plan must Contain Specific Deadlines For All Milestones to Achieving the End

Set realistic deadlines or time targets, and always keep them in perspective, probably through fixed dates, time or targeted goals.

To everything there is a season and a time to every purpose under heaven. A time to be born, a tie to die, a time to plant and a time to pluck up that which is planted. A time to kill and a time to heal, a time to break down, and a time to build up. A time to weep and a time to laugh; a time to mourn and a time to dance; A time to cast away stones, and a time to gather stones together; a time to embrace, and a time to refrain from embracing. A time to get and a time to loose, a time to keep and a time to cast away. A time to rend, and a time to sew; a time to keep silence, and a time to speak; A time to love and a time to hate, a time of war, and a time of peace.[10]

---

[10] *Ecclesiastes 3:1-8*

Chapter 7

Ministry and Finance

Cry yet saying, thus saith the LORD of hosts, my cities through prosperity shall yet be spread abroad; and the LORD shall yet comfort Zion, and shall yet choose Jerusalem.[1]

Ministry Can neither Excel nor Succeed without Finance

Impact is not just the product of the anointing or the Word, but also the amount of fund you have to push it. The spread of the Gospel is made easy and faster through finance. The more finance you have, the greater the opportunities to advance your cause.

[13] *This wisdom have I seen under the sun, and it seemed great unto me;* [14]*There was a little city, and few men within it, and there came a great king against it and besieged it, and built great bulwarks against it.* [15]*Now there was found in it a poor wise man, and he by wisdom delivered the city, yet no man remembered that same poor man.* [16] *Then said I, Wisdom is better than strength, nevertheless the poor man's wisdom is despised, and his words are not heard.*[2]

A man can have a great, unique and excellent idea, concept or even vision, but the lack of the necessary funds needed to push it could cripple it.

---

[1] Zechariah 1:17
[2] Eccl 9:13-16

Please understand that anointing without money leads to frustration and annoyance.

When You Don't Have Finance, Make Sure You Have Wisdom.

You can never be wise and not prosper. One of the true evidence of wisdom is prosperity.

[11]Wisdom is good with an inheritance, and by it there is profit to them that see the sun. [12] For wisdom is a defence, and money is a defence; but excellency of knowledge is, that wisdom giveth life to them that have it.[3]

Many people or ministers don't have money problems but wisdom problems.

Better is a poor and wise child than an old and foolish king, who will no more be admonished.[4]

You can always attract what you don't have. Wisdom brings an inner strength.

Who is a wise man? And who knoweth the interpretation of a thing? A man's wisdom maketh his face to shine, and the boldness of his face shall be changed.[5]

What is wisdom?

Wisdom is knowing the interpretation of any matter.

Hear instruction and be wise, and refuse it not.[6]

---

[3] Ecclesiastes 7:11-12
[4] Ecclesiastes 4:13
[5] Ecclesiastes 7:19
[6] Proverbs 8:33

Ministry is Spiritual Business

Wherefore, brethren, look ye out among you seven men of honest report, full of the Holy Ghost and wisdom, whom we may appoint over this business.[7]

Most people in ministry do not excel because they take ministry casually. When we talk about business, we talk about investment and profit.

And he said unto them, how is it that ye sought me? Wist ye not that I must be about my Father's business?[8]

When you have this understanding, your approach will change because it is foolishness to do something that is not profitable.

Things that will Aid Us in This Kingdom Business are:

(a) The Gospel Business Demands Diligence

Proverbs. 22:29 - *Seest thou a man diligent in his business? He shall stand before kings; he shall not stand before mere men.*

Your diligence determines or controls the level you get into and where you stand. The opposite of diligence is slothfulness.

Romans 12:11 - *Not slothful in business, fervent in spirit, serving the Lord;* KJV

Diligence talks of:

i. **Fervency**: This is maintaining zeal from boiling point-turnover point.

The word diligence also means:

ii. **Service:** This is using your life to achieve an aim. Each time you serve, there is profit.

Exodus 23:25 - *And ye shall serve the LORD your God, and he shall bless*

---
[7] Acts 6:3
[8] Luke 2:49

thy bread, and thy water; and I will take sickness away from the midst of thee.

Only few individuals actually use their lives, time, energy, resources to achieve an aim especially when they are not personally involved.

(b) Consistent Hard Work

Psalm 107:23-31 - [23] *They that go down to the sea in ships, that do business in great waters;* [24] *These see the works of the LORD, and his wonders in the deep.* [25] *For he commandeth, and raiseth the stormy wind, which lifteth up waves thereof.* [26] *They mount up to the heaven, they go down again to the depths, their soul is melted because of trouble.* [27] *They reel to and fro, and stagger like a drunken man, and are at wit's end.* [28] *Then they cry unto the LORD in their trouble, and he bringeth them out of their distresses.* [29] *He maketh the storm a calm, so that the waves therof are still.* [30] *Then they are glad because they be quiet; so he bringeth them into their desired haven.*

Hard work is not work if it is not consistent, steady and continuous. It is not about working hard for a while, but remaining hard working.

Avoid Waste

John 6:12- *When they were filled, he said unto his disciples, gather up the fragments that remain, that nothing be lost.*

Matthew 14:15-20 - [15] *And when it was evening, his disciples came to him saying, this is a desert place, and the time is now past, send the multitude away, that they may go into the villages and buy themselves victuals.* [16] *But Jesus said unto them, they need not depart, give ye them to eat.* [17] *And they say unto him, we have here, five loaves and two fishes.* [18] *He said, bring them hither to me* [19] *And he commanded the multitude to sit down on the grass, and he took the five loaves, and the two fishes, and looking up to heaven, he blessed, brake, and gave the five loaves to his disciples, and the disciples to the multitude.* [20] *And they did all eat, and were filled; and they took up of the fragments that remained.*

Waste products are always raw materials for reproduction; so always be mindful of the remains, leftovers or wastes, because they are always there.

Matthew 26:8- *But when his disciples saw it, they had indignation, saying, to what purpose is this waste?*

Every waste has a purpose in ministry. Always discover the purpose. Discover what people in ministry waste. Discover the purpose because the waste is always the multiplied fragment of your resources.

In ministry, managing your resources includes managing your waste.

Proverbs 18:9- *He also that is slothful in his work is brother to him that is a great waster.*

Association plays a major role in one's success.

One of the things that cause waste is slothfulness.

Luke 15:12-13 - *[12] And the younger of them said to his father, father, give me the portion of goods that falleth to me. And he divided unto them his living. [13] And not many days after, the younger son gathered all together and took his journey into a far country, and there wasted his substance with riotous living.*

When we talk about waste, it's talking about wasting your life, destiny and future. If you must avoid waste, you must cut down costs, your way of life and associations because there are always people that will spur you to waste your money, gifts, energy, and time. When these things are wasted, finance and substance is wasted. Only what is necessary should be used or released.

You Must Network to Prosper

Ecclesiastes 4:9-11 - *[9] Two are better than one, because they have a good reward for their labour. [10] For if they fall, the one will lift up his fellow, but woe to him that is alone when he falleth, for he hath not another to help him up. [11] Again, if two lie together, then they have heat, but how can one be warm alone?*

Don't labour alone in ministry. One of the things we need to excel is connection. It enhances labour for productivity.

Ecclesiastes 10:15- *The labour of the foolish wearieth every one of them, because he knoweth not how to go to the city.*

Labour without relevant connection leads to frustration.

Acts 8:30-31 - *³⁰ And Philip ran thither to him and heard him read the prophet Esaias and said, understandeth thou what thou readest? ³¹ And he said, how can I, except some man should guide me? And he desired Philip that he would come up and sit with him.*

Identify who your co-labourers are. It is wisdom to know those who subtract from your life and avoid them.

Proverbs. 28:29 - *He that tilleth his land shall have plenty of bread; but he that followeth after vain persons shall have poverty enough.*

To Make Money, Work is Needed

Ecclesiastes 4:5- *The fool foldeth his hands together, and eateth his own flesh.*

Proverbs. 13:23- *The soul of the sluggard desireth and hath nothing, but the soul of the diligent shall be made fat.*

Proverbs 24:30-34 - *³⁰ I went by the field of the slothful, and by the vineyard of the man void of understanding.³¹ And lo, it was all grown over with thorns, and nettles had covered the face thereof, and the stone wall thereof was broken down. ³² Then I saw and considered it well, I looked upon it, and it received instruction. ³³ Yet a little sleep a little slumber, a little folding of the hands to sleep ³⁴ So shall thy poverty come as one that travelleth, and thy want as an armed man.*

Before you eat each day, check how much you earn.

Genesis 2:2- *And on the seventh day God ended his work which he had made and rested on the seventh day from all his work which he has made.*

TO MAKE MONEY, WORK IS NEEDED

Don't rest until you finish all the work.

Whatsoever thy hand findeth to do, do with all thy might, for there is no work, nor device, nor knowledge, nor wisdom in the grave whither thou goes.

Work is needed to make money. Work is defined as the ability to reproduce what you have.

Proverbs 12:27- *The slothful man roasteth not that which he took in hunting, but the substance of a diligent man is precious.*

Work is also defined as an ability to use your potentials positively for production.

Matthew 25:14-15 - *¹⁴ For the kingdom of heaven is as a man travelling into a far country, who called his own servants, and delivered unto them his goods. ¹⁵ And unto one he gave five talents, to another tow and to another one, to every man according to his several ability; and straightway took his journey.*

Luke 19:12-14 - *¹² He said therefore, a certain noble man went into a far country to receive for himself a kingdom, and to return. ¹³ And he called his ten servants, and delivered them ten pounds and said unto them, occupy till I come. ¹⁴ But his citizens hated him and sent a messenger after him saying, we will not have this man to reign over us.*

Deuteronomy 32:4- *He is the Rock, his work is perfect for all his ways are judgement; a God of truth and without iniquity, just and right.*

Don't just work but make sure that your work is perfect, beautiful and excellent.

Proverbs 27:23-27 - *²³ Be thou diligent to know the state of thy flocks and look well to the herds. ²⁴ For riches are not forever; and doth the crown endure to every generation? ²⁵ The hay appeareth and the tender grass sheweth itself and herbs of the mountains are gathered. ²⁶ The lambs for thy clothing and the goats are the price of the field. ²⁷ And thou shalt have goat's milk enough for thy food of thy household and for the maintenance for thy maidens.*

Your level of work determines what you enjoy because work has to come before pleasure.

You Must Give Away Poverty

Your calling into ministry also entails that you must give away poverty. You are not only supposed to be at the receiving end, but you should also position yourself at the giving end. What ministers expect others to do to prosper financially they must also do, and this includes: Tithing, Seed Sowing, Thanksgiving Offering, Prophet's Offering, Offering, Vows, etc.

There are some strong secrets that can inspire you to give in ministry. They are:

Ecclesiastes 11:1-6 - *^{1}Cast thy bread upon many waters, for thou shalt find it after many days. ^{2}Give a portion to seven, and also to eight, for thou knowest not what evil shall be upon the earth. ^{3}If the clouds be full of rain, they empty themselves upon the earth; and if the tree fall toward the south, or toward the north, in the place where tree falleth, there it shall be. ^{4}He that observeth the wind shall not sow, and he that regardeth the clouds shall not reap. ^{5}As thou knowest not what is the way of the spirit, nor how the bones do grow in the womb of her that is with child, even so thou knowest not the works of God who maketh all. ^{6}In the morning sow thy seed, and in the evening withhold not.*

Genesis 22:17-18 - *^{17}That in blessing I will bless thee, and in multiplying, I will multiply thy seed as the stars of heaven; and as the sand which is upon the seashore, and thy seed shall possess the gate of his enemies. ^{18}And in thy seed shall all the nations of the earth be blessed, because thou hast obeyed my voice.*

Most often you give out of your comfort; but this is no proper.

Giving must be generous. Everyone around us ought to benefit from our giving, in one way or the other.

Know the Rewarder

Hebrews 11:6- *But without faith it is impossible to please Him, for he that cometh to God must believe that he is, and that he is a rewarder of them that diligently seek him.*

You must also know that no man can reward you for what you are doing. There is a limit to what an individual can offer you. Men can give you and get tired of giving, but when God gives he cannot end. God is an endless supplier. He is never exhausted and can raise anyone to give or bless you.

Esther 6:1- *On that night could not the king sleep, and he commanded to bring the book of records of the chronicles and they were read before the king.*

In ministry, one of the greatest mistakes we make is we move our eyes away from God and we look at men as the supplier. God is the rewarder, the Church or men are not our rewarder.

Genesis 15:1- *After these things, the word of the LORD came to Abram in a vision saying, fear not, Abram, I am thy shield and thy exceeding great reward.*

Don't Be in Haste (Patience)

Proverbs. 28:20

It is important to note that haste will lead you into compromise for more money or members

1 Timothy 6:6- *But godliness with contentment is great gain.*

Job 14:14- *If a man die, shall he live again? All the days of my appointed time will I wait, till my change come.*

To be prosperous and have your membership increase, do not be in haste. You are not in a competition with anybody.

Romans 9:33- *As it is written, behold I lay in Sion a stumbling stone and*

rock of offence, and whosoever believeth on him shall not be ashamed.

It means that haste leads to shame. Haste is an indication of lack of faith in God. If you have faith in the promise, you will not make haste.

When you must have done your part, leave the rest to God. This is essential as sometimes your best is not seen as good enough by your members (subjects)

Luke 8:15- But that on the good ground are they, which in an honest and good heart, having heard the word, keep it and bring forth fruit with patience.

Patience shows how good your heart is.

Luke 6:12- That ye be not slothful but followers of them who through faith and patience inherit the promises.

To inherit the promise (riches, wealth, etc,) you need the virtue of patience. It is a virtue; you have to develop it.

Romans 8:23-25 - [23] And not only they, but ourselves also which have the first fruits of the Spirit, even we ourselves groan within ourselves waiting for adoption, to wit, the redemption of our body. [24] For we are saved by hope, but hope that is seen is not hope; for what a man seeth, why doth he yet hope? [25] But if we hope for that we see not, then do we with patience wait for it.

Any man that is in haste has no hope. The virtue of patience keeps you focused. A man of focus is a man void of distractions. You must keep your eyes on the promise. For every patient man there must be a promise in perspective.

James 1:3- Knowing this, that the trying of your faith worketh patience.

Go for the Blessing

If you want to prosper in ministry, your greatest target or goal should be the blessing.

Proverbs 10:22- The blessing of the LORD, it maketh rich and he addeth

GO FOR THE BLESSING

no sorrow with it.

Don't go for the riches, go for the blessing.

Genesis 12:1-3 - *¹ Now the Lord had said unto Abram, get thee out of thy country, and from thy kindred and from thy father's house, unto a land that I will shew thee. ² And I will make of thee a great nation, and I will bless thee, and make thy name great; and thou shalt be a blessing. ³ And I will bless them that bless thee, and curse him that curseth thee; and in thee shall all the families of the earth be blessed.*

Abraham transcended the level of being blessed to becoming the blessing himself; the blessing of the Lord.

Genesis 28:1-4 - *¹ And Isaac called Jacob and blessed him and charged him, and said to unto him, Thou shall not take a wife of the daughters of Canaan,² Arise, go to Padan Aram, to the house of Bethuel, thy mother's father, and take thee a wife from thence of the daughters of Laban, thy mother's brother. ³ And God Almighty bless thee, and make thee fruitful and multiply thee; that thou mayest be a multitude of people; ⁴ And give thee the blessing of Abraham to thee, and to thy seed with thee, that thou mayest inherit the land wherein thou art a stranger, which God gave unto Abraham.*

This reference above *"The Blessing of the Lord"* is a covenant instruction given to an individual by God which has consequent reward. For every man God blessed, there was a token of covenant. The blessing is the exchange of the tokens of the token that produces riches. So, under an anointing, go for your own blessing (covenant instructions)

Be careful about operating with a blessing you are not conscious of. This indicates a consciousness of what the covenant instructions are and the consequent reward; because until obedience is complete, disobedience cannot be revenged.

2 Corinthians. 10:6- *And having in a readiness to revenge all disobedience, when your obedience is fulfilled.*

Chapter 8

The Making of a Pastor

And I will give you pastors according to mine heart, which shall feed you with knowledge and understanding.[1]

God's gift to the world is Jesus, while the gift of Jesus' to the church is the five-fold ministry.

As a Pastor, you are a gift to the body of Christ. After Jesus, you are the next gift. So you ought to be the perfect representation of Jesus on earth.

Now then we are ambassadors for Christ as though God did beseech you by us, we pray you in Christ's stead, be ye reconciled to God.[2]

The making of a Pastor is a serious responsibility.

5 Keywords in the Making of a Pastor

In the making of a Pastor, you will consider the key words, 'FOLLOW', 'I', 'MAKE', 'MEN'.

1. Follow

Has to do with sheep. In becoming great you need to be foolish in following God or following his servants. If you cannot surrender, you can't be made. In leadership, an individual must be able to trust and

---

[1] Jeremiah 3:15
[2] 2 Corinthians. 5:20

love the leader with his or her whole life.

2. 'I'

Represents Mentorship or Leadership or Spiritual Authority.

Be ye therefore followers of God as dear children[3]

Be ye followers of me, even as I also am of Christ.[4]

In leadership, you follow a man, the supposed way you'll follow God if you see him physically.

3. Make

It is a process of change or transformation or metamorphosis from one state to the other.

In leadership, both you and the mentor should know that you are a raw material. You must understand how the mentor's mind works. If you don't understand the point of making, you will not follow the leadership effectively. The making should be a dual process. Your mentor assumes the place of a trainer in the process. He has the responsibility of moving you from your present state to where God wants you to be.

4. Men

Talks about scope of influence or authority.

After the making, there is a desired position and there are responsibilities that should be committed into your hand. You cannot carry these responsibilities except you are made. You cannot lead without making sacrifices.

There are two purposes for being made

Howbeit for this cause I obtained mercy, that in me, first Jesus Christ shew forth all longsuffering, for a pattern to them which should

---

[3] Ephesians 5:1
[4] 1 Corinthians.11:1

hereafter believe on him to life everlasting.⁵

1. So that Christians be filled with love that comes from a pure heart, a clear conscience and sincere faith. (Pure love is lacking in the body of Christ, so this is the first purpose for which you are called as a Pastor- that you'll bring love among the people)

2. So that our lives can be used as a prime example of his great patience, grace, mercy and love.

The process of being made entails responsibility in 5 domains

Domain 1: Responsibilities towards God

You are being made for God's use and your responsibilities towards God are as follows:

(a) Clinging tight to your faith

Holding faith, and a good conscience, which some having put away concerning faith have made shipwreck.⁶

Fight the good fight of faith, lay hold on eternal life, whereunto thou art called, and hast professed a good profession before many witnesses.⁷

Hold fast the form of sound words, which thou has heard of me, in faith and in love which is in Christ Jesus. That good thing which was committed unto thee, keep by the Holy Ghost which dwelleth in you.⁸

But continue on the things which thou hast learned and be assured of, knowing whom thou hast learned them.⁹

It is a responsibility to hold to your faith. It is very important because the

---

[5] 1 Timothy 1:16
[6] 1 Timothy 1:19
[7] 1 Timothy 6:12
[8] 2 Timothy 1:13-14
[9] 11 Timothy 3:14

moment your faith in God drops, you will become shipwrecked or fall.

(b) Prayer

Exhort therefore, that, first of all, supplications, prayers, intercessions, and giving thanks, be made for all men; For kings, and for all that are in authority, that we may lead a quiet peaceable life in all godliness and honesty. [10]

It is a responsibility that we have, to talk with God. Jesus practically lived a life of prayer. He always prayed before he came out to manifest. He prayed in the night and manifested in the day. If you don't pray effectively, you cannot manifest effectively.

(c) Godly exercise

But refuse profane and old wives' fables, and exercise thyself rather unto godliness. [11]

Spend time and energy training yourself in spiritual things, for example, choosing your words, choosing where to go, building godly relationships. One must be conscious of the things that make Christians godly, for example, greetings, how you smile, your decisions and exercise godliness in judgement (looking into the part of your life that is not in tune with the statutes of God and working on them).

(d) Obedience

Now these things were our example, to the intent that we should not lust after evil things, as they also lusted. [12]

The devil cannot respect you, if you are not faithful in obedience. I cannot avenge disobedience, if I am disobedient because these forces know our level of obedience in Christ. [13]

You cannot cast out a devil when you have the devil in you.

---

[10] 1 Timothy 2:1-2
[11] 1 Timothy 4:7
[12] 1 Corinthians 10:6
[13] 2 Corinthians 10:6

Whereupon King Agrippa, I was not disobedient unto the heavenly vision.[14]

It is your responsibility to obey instructions and commands from God. Your obedience to God must be complete. It is part of your responsibility towards God. We don't see certain results in our lives because of our disobedience to God.

You cannot lead people that are much more committed to God than you.

(e) Availability for service

But in a great house there are not only vessels of gold and of silver, but also of wood and of earth, and some to honour and some to dishonour. If a man therefore purge himself from these, he shall be a vessel unto honour, sanctified and meet for the master's use, and prepared unto every good work.[15]

But watch thou in all things, endure afflictions, do the work of an evangelist, make full proof of thy ministry.[16]

3 Major Ways to Be Available

i. If you are to be available for services, you must purge yourself to be a vessel. It means your ability to get rid of things that will prevent you from being used.

ii. Be available by becoming apt to teach.

iii. Always be present so people can always reach you at any time. It is a disappointment to God when you are not always available to meet people's needs.

Not forsaking the assembling of ourselves together, as the manner of some is, but exhorting one another, and so much the more, as ye see the day approaching.[17]

---

[14] Acts 26:19
[15] 2 Timothy 2:20-21
[16] 2 Timothy 4:5
[17] Hebrews 10:25

(f) Respect your spiritual authority

Put them in mind to be subject to principalities and powers, to obey magistrates, to be ready to every good work. To speak evil of no man, to be no brawlers, but gentle, shewing all meekness unto all men. [18]

It is my spiritual responsibility towards God to respect my spiritual authority. The tongue, the heart, the mouth must be covenanted to respect the anointed.

Let every soul be subject to the governing authorities. For there is no authority except from God, and the authorities that exist are appointed by God. Therefore, whoever resists the authority resists the ordinance of God, and those who resist will bring judgment on themselves. For rulers are not a terror to good works but to evil. Do you want to be unafraid of the authority? Do what is good, and you will have praise from the same. For he is God's minister to you for good. But if you do evil, be afraid; for he does not bear the sword in vain; for He is God's minister, an avenger to execute wrath on him who practices evil.[19]

So David and Abishai came to the people by night, and there Saul lay sleeping within the camp, with his spear stuck in the ground by his head. And Abner and the people lay all around him. Then Abishai said to David, "God has delivered your enemy into your hand this day. Now therefore, please, let me strike him at once with the spear, right to the earth; and I will not have to strike him a second time!" But David said to Abishai, "Do not destroy him, for who can stretch out his hand against the LORD'S anointed, and be guiltless? David said furthermore, "As the LORD lives, the LORD shall strike him, or his day shall come to die or he shall go out to battle and perish. The Lord forbid that I should stretch out my hand against the LORD'S anointed. But please, take now the spear and the jug of water that are by his head, and let us go".[20]

Then the men of David said to him, " This is the day of which the LORD said to you, 'Behold I will deliver your enemy into your hand, that you may do to him as it seems good to you. "And David arose and secretly cut off a corner of Saul's robe. Now it happened afterward that David's

---

[18] Titus 3:1-2
[19] Romans 13:1-4
[20] 1 Samuel 26:7-11

heart troubled him because he had cut Saul's robe. And he said to his men, " The LORD forbid that I should do this thing to my master, the LORD's anointed, to stretch out my hand against him, seeing he is the anointed of the LORD. ⁷ So David restrained his servants with these words and did not allow them to rise against Saul. And Saul got up from the cave and went on his way.²¹

Our faith in Jesus is tested by our faith in the people around us. If we can't respect the authority we see, then we can't respect the authority of God; 1 John 4:20. We can't say we love God when we do not love our brother whom we see.

Domain 2: Responsibilities towards the Church

(a) Being an example (role model)

1 Timothy 4:12- Let no man despise thy youth, but be thou an example of the believers, in word, in conversation, in charity, in spirit, in faith, in purity.

Every Pastor has a responsibility to show people the way first by their actions.

Acts 1:1- We should all learn not to teach what we have not done or do not do.

Titus 2:1-8-¹ But speak thou the things which become sound doctrine. ²That the aged men be sober, grave, temperate, sound in faith, in charity, in patience. ³The aged women likewise, that they be in behaviour as becometh holiness, not false accusers, not given to much wine, teachers of good things. ⁴ That they may teach the young women to be sober, to love their husbands, to love their children; ⁵ To be discreet, chaste, keepers at home, good, obedient to their own husbands, that the Word of God be not blasphemed. ⁶ Young men likewise exhort to be sober minded. ⁷ In all things shewing thyself a pattern of good works, in doctrine shewing uncorruptness, gravity, sincerity,⁸Sound speech, that cannot be condemned, that he that is of the contrary part may be ashamed, having no evil thing to say of you.

---

[21] 1 Samuel 24:4-7

Part of leadership responsibility is to live above flaws and faults so that men will be challenged/inspired that there is no corrupt thing in you, i.e. to live above the flaws of men.

To be an example is not a function of age but your ability to develop yourself to be a role model. If you have nobody looking up to you, your life should be questioned.

(b) Read, encourage and teach the church

1 Timothy 4:13- Till I come, give attendance to reading, to exhortation, to doctrine.

2 Timothy 4:2- *Preach the word! Be ready in season and out of season. Convince, rebuke, exhort, with all longsuffering and teaching.*

There is always a standard in ministry. The Gospel has a standard, and so also should every man of God, there should be no compromise. By being taught and rebuked, you are brought up to the required standard. You pull the people from where they are to where you are through teaching, reproof, rebuke, counsel and correction.

See Titus 2:1-8

It is your responsibility to teach the church good things and before you teach, you must be well read and also a role model.

(c) Utilize and appropriate your gifts

1 Timothy 4:14-16-[14] *Neglect not the gift that is in thee, which was given thee by prophecy, with the laying on of hands of the presbytery.* [15] *Meditate upon these things; give thyself wholly to them, that thy profiting may appear to all.* [16] *Take heed unto thyself, and unto the doctrine, continue in them, for in doing so this thou shalt both save thyself and them that hear thee.*

2 Timothy 1:6- *Therefore, do not be ashamed of the testimony of our Lord, nor of me His prisoner, but share with me in the sufferings for the gospel according to the power of God.*

Your gift is an essential tool for ministry. Your gift makes ministry easy and more effective. When you do ministry with gifts and without gifts, the difference is usually obvious.

Utilizing or using your gift is necessary for ministry, so stir up your gifts. If it is not stirred, it will be dormant, ineffective and unproductive.

Ways To Stir Up Your Gifts Are:

i. *Prayer and fasting*:
Our emphasis is not just on talents, but on spiritual gift. (1 Corinthians 12:1-12) For it to come to full manifestation, prayer and fasting become a must, basically because these gifts are spiritual and not natural.

ii. *Exercising to use the gifts*:
To exercise is to train, rehearse or practice your gifts and this deals basically with both natural and spiritual gifts.

(d) Endure suffering

2 Timothy 2:3-4- *² Thou therefore endure hardness, as a good soldier of Jesus Christ. ³ No man that warreth entangleth himself with the affairs of this life; that he may please him who hath chosen him to be a soldier.*

Ministry is military; enduring hardship is part of your Christian responsibility. To be a blessing to people will definitely cost you a lot.

1 Peter 3:14-18- *14 But even if you should suffer for righteousness' sake, you are blessed. " And do not be afraid of their threats, nor be troubled". 15 But sanctify the Lord God in your hearts, and always be ready to give a defense to everyone who asks you a reason for the hope that is in you, with meekness and fear; 16 Having a good conscience, that when they defame you as evildoers, those who revile your good conduct in Christ may be ashamed. 17 For it is better, if it is the will of God, to suffer for doing good than doing evil. 18 For Christ also suffered once for sins, the just for the unjust, that he might bring us to God, being put to death in the flesh but made alive by the Spirit. NKJV*

Learn to suffer hardness as a good soldier of Jesus Christ. Most believers don't understand and value the place of suffering for the Gospel. So then it has become a major issue where Christians shy away from their spiritual obligations towards the people around them, all because no one wants to be nailed for what he believes.

(e) Warfare

2 Timothy 2:4- *No man that warreth entangleth himself with this affairs of this life, that he may please him who hath chosen him to be a soldier.*

Ministry is warfare, and the Pastor must understand that the ministry of the Gospel is a battlefield. It is a job where you contend with spiritual forces more and in warfare, there are winners and losers.

1 Timothy 6:12- *Fight the good fight of faith, lay hold on eternal life, to which you were also called and have confessed the good confession in the presence of many witnesses. NKJV*

(f) hardwork

2 Timothy 2:6- *The husbandman that laboureth must first be partaker of the fruits.*

You must understand that labour comes before enjoyment.

Matthew 9:37-38- *³⁷ Then He said to His disciples, "The harvest is plentiful, but the labourers are few". ³⁸ Therefore pray the Lord of harvest to send out labourers into His harvest".*

Your responsibility is to work hard in being a labourer.

John 5:17- *"My father worketh hither I work".*

As a Pastor, always bear this in mind that there is no substitute for hard work, so the issue of hard work can never be over emphasized in ministry. A lot of ministers and ministries failed and the blame went to satanic attacks, while if you get down to the root cause, you will discover that the pastor is lazy, passive, slothful, not serious or even reluctant about the ministerial demands.

(g) Institute leadership

Titus 1:5- *For this reason I left you in Crete, that you should set in* order the things that are lacking, and appoint elders in every city as I commanded you.

Bring in order and organization wherever you are.

Acts 6:3-Therefore, brethren seek out from among you seven men of good reputation, full of the Holy Spirit and wisdom, whom you may appoint over this business.

Mark 3:14- Then He appointed twelve, that they might be with him and that He might send them out to preach.

2 Timothy 2:2- And the things that you have heard from me among many witnesses, commit these to faithful men who will be able to teach others also. NKJV

Consciously train and appoint men and women who believe in the work to be in charge of details as they are being put in place, because this determines and guarantees establishment.

(h) Charitable

Colossians 3:14- But above all these things put on love, which is the bond of perfection. NKJV

See 1 Corinthians 13

James 1:27- Pure and undefiled before God and the Father is this, to visit the father less and widows in their affliction, and to keep himself unspotted from the world.

Pure Christianity is charitable-that is, it embodies the act of charity. As a minister you must exhibit the act of charity. Selfless attention should be given to all individuals, who are privileged to come in contact with your ministry, and let it be without the expectation that your reward come from the people you have helped. Focus on showing charity rather.

Domain 3: Responsibility towards Fellow Believers

(a) Respect

1 Timothy 5:1-3- *¹ Do not rebuke an older man, but exhort him as a father, younger men as brothers,² older women as mothers, younger women as sisters, with all purity. ³ Honour widows who really are widows. NKJV*

Luke 9:46-50- *Then a dispute arose among them as to which of them would be the greatest.*

As a Pastor, you should have respect for other people's calling, grace, convictions, and individual ideology. Respect other people's views. You should not castigate ministers, though you may not accept or imbibe the concept of a ministry or a minister, you must respect them.

(b) Good administration or relationship

1 Timothy 5:19-20- *¹⁹ Do not receive an accusation against an elder except from two or three witnesses. ²⁰ Those who are sinning rebuke in the presence of all, that the rest also may fear. NKJV*

Good administration is important for a balanced ministry. You must be able to proffer solutions to problems and issues. Know what to do at every given time. You must also know when to reject people and when to accept others because in leadership, there must be an understanding that all persons must not serve under your ministry. This understanding gives you a very liberal attitude towards people, especially the way they react or relate with your ministry. Give everyone who sincerely believes in what you are doing the opportunity to get involved without feeling insecure in any way.

(c) Avoid favouritism

You must treat everybody equally. Visits, commitments, out reaches and decisions taken in your administration should not be biased or partial (See James 2:1-9). Everyone must be accommodated and allowed to fit into your system.

Domain 4: Responsibility towards Yourself

(a) Don't limit yourself

1 Timothy 4:12- *Let no one despise your youth, but be an example to the believers in the word, in conduct, in love, in spirit, in faith, in purity. NKJV*

Titus 2:15- *These, then, are the things you should teach. Encourage and rebuke with all authority. Do not let anyone despise you.*

Don't allow people despise you irrespective of their level of affluence, education or wealth. To achieve this, you must develop yourself to be an example.

Don't Despise Yourself (Low self esteem). Don't limit yourself. You cannot go beyond your faith in yourself. Learn not to look down, undermine or despise yourself. Don't underrate or underestimate yourself.

Be A Pacesetter. Be an example, a positive reference point. Be the best among those you are leading, do things that others will emulate, do things that others will like to imitate because people should emulate you and look up to you.

(b) Avoid compromise

1 Timothy 5:22- *Do not lay hands on anyone hastily, nor share in other people's sins; keep yourself pure.*

1 Timothy 6:11- *But you, O man of God, flee these things and pursue righteousness, godliness, faith, love, patience, gentleness.*

2 Timothy 2:19-22- [19] *Nevertheless the solid foundation of God stands, having this seal: "The Lord knows who are His, "and, "Let everyone who names the name of Christ depart from iniquity".* [20] *But in a great house there are not only vessels of gold and silver, but also of wood and clay, some for honour and some for dishonour.* [21] *Therefore if any one cleanses himself from the latter, he will be a vessel for honour, sanctified and useful for every good work.* [22] *Flee also youthful lusts; pursue righteousness, faith, love, peace with those who call on the Lord out of a pure heart. NKJV*

You must discover areas where you must not compromise your standard; and as a leader, you must have principles that people should not break, e.g. purity, sanity, righteousness and holiness above all, should be paramount in your life. You should develop them as a mentality.

(c) Be content

1 Timothy 6:6-8- *⁶ Now godliness with contentment is great gain. ⁷ For we brought nothing into this world, and it is certain we can carry nothing out. ⁸ And having food and clothing, with these we shall be content. NKJV*

Be content with whatever you have and be thankful to God for every level at which you find yourself. Life is always a process and you must start from somewhere; growth is constant in life. We should learn to be content rather than living a false life.

(d) Avoid the love of money and covetousness

1 Timothy 6:10- *For the love of money is a root of all kinds of evil, for which some have strayed from the faith in their greediness; and pierced themselves through with many sorrows.*

The love of money makes you not give out. Develop giving as a principle. You need money but don't love it; if you love money, you can't have it or release it.

(e) Stir or activate your gift

2 Timothy 1:6- *Therefore I remind you to stir up the gift of God which is in you through the laying on of my hands.*

First discover your gifting and stir up your gifts. And gift not used lies dormant and does not grow. There is a grace that comes by performance. Put your gift to use, train yourself. Spend time to train yourself.

(f) Boldness

2 Timothy 1:7-8- *⁷ For God has not given us a spirit of fear but of power and of love and of a sound mind. ⁸ Therefore do not be ashamed of the* testimony of our Lord, nor of me His prisoner, but share with me in the sufferings for the gospel according to the power of God.

2 Timothy 2:1- You therefore, my son, be strong in the grace that is in Christ Jesus. Be confident in your grace and gifting. Boldness comes by the Holy Spirit:

Acts 4:31- And when they had prayed, the place where they were assembled together was shaken; and they were filled with the Holy Spirit, and they spoke the word of God with boldness. NKJV

To handle matters you need boldness. For you to be bold, you should pray for the Holy Ghost to be present in your matters.

11 Timothy 2:12- And when they had prayed, the place where they were assembled together was shaken, and they were all filled with the Holy Spirit, and they spake the Word of God with boldness.

Acts 2:12- So they were all amazed and perplexed, saying to one another, "Whatsoever could this mean"?

You need boldness in several situations to stand for Christ. Boldness is rising in the face of adversities.

(g) Die to self

2 Timothy 2:11- Cretans and Arabs- we hear them speaking in our own tongues the wonderful works of God.

You must learn to think less of yourself (selfless) to come out excellent as a minster. Suffering is part of my Christian package. You must overlook the pleasures and material things around you. You must be open to insults and humiliation and attacks in your ministry because they must come. To be an effective minister, you must learn to be selfless like Paul. Be sacrificial; you cannot serve God effectively while you are still alive in the flesh.

See 2 Corinthians. 11:16-27

(h) Avoid bad company

11 Timothy 2:16-17- *[16] But shun profane and idle babblings for they will increase to more ungodliness. [17] And their message will spread like cancer; Hymenaeus and Philetus are of this sort. NKJV*

Your faith can be overthrown by people around you. Be nice to all but you cannot maintain every relationship. In ministry, it is better to break relationships early than drag them. If a friend does not meet your standard in Christ, you must stop the friendship. You must always evaluate your relationships; break off with ungodly and scornful sinners when people don't meet up with your standard in life. Company is very important.

(i) Good character

Developing a good character is your responsibility and not the responsibility of your father or Pastor. It is not imparted by someone; you have to decide to build your character. Learn to build your character for your future.

2 Timothy 2:21- *Therefore if anyone cleanses himself from the latter, he will be a vessel for honour, sanctified and useful for the Master, prepared for every good work. NKJV*

Write out things you want to do and list out things you are doing you don't like. The development of a good character can only come if a child sees reasons to change. The best way to develop good character is to consciously change or correct the bad ones.

(j) Physical appearance

1 Timothy 2:9-10- *[9] In like manner also, that the women adorn themselves in modest apparel, with propriety and moderation, not with braided hair or gold or costly clothing, [10] but, which is proper for women professing godliness, with good works.*

Your physical appearance says a lot about you. The way you look and dress is very important.

Domain 5: Responsibility towards Your Home

Rightfully assume responsibility at home first and then the church; (1Timothy 3:1-12)

1Timothy 5:8- *But if anyone does not provide for his own, and especially for those of his household, he has denied the faith and is worse than an unbeliever. NKJV*

Be of good behaviour, blameless, and hospitable. Whatever is your role, husband, wife, son, daughter, etc. Assume your rightful place in the house.

Chapter 9

Jethro's Principles

Leadership is not about titles or positions but influence. Saul was King but David was leading.[1] As they say, it is not the hood that makes the monk. It is a wrong to just bear titles or associate names with leadership. Leadership means carrying responsibilities. David did not become capable because he was made king. Being ordained is not the only requirement to be successful as a pastor but also your ability to shoulder responsibilities.

Leaders are made, not born! Nobody is born to lead. God can use anything to make you. Leadership is a calling or conviction from God especially when it has to do with spiritual things. If you do not have a calling or conviction, you will struggle in leadership. From struggling to confusion, to frustration, to retrogression, and of course, quitting.

Leadership is simply using influence to achieve a goal or set of goals by working with people. When the people you are leading are not responsive, you are not an effective leader. While Saul was king, the people were responding to David. Influence is not by force, it is by impact; influence and impact are major in leadership.

Read Exodus 18:1-27

[1] And Jethro, the Priest of Midian, Moses' father in-law, heard of all that God had done for Moses and for Israel His people- that the LORD had brought Israel out of Egypt.[2] The Jethro Moses' father in-law took Zipporah, Moses' wife, after he had sent her back. [3] With her two sons

---
[1] 2 Samuel 5:2

of whom the name of one was Gershom (for he said, "I have been a stranger in a foreign land") ⁴ And the name of the other was Eliezer (for he said, "The God of my father was my help, and delivered me from the sword of Pharaoh");⁵ And Jethro, Moses' father in-law, came with his sons and his wife to Moses in the wilderness, where he encamped at the mountain of God.⁶ Now he said to Moses, "I, your father in-law Jethro, am coming to you with your wife and her two sons with her".

⁷ So Moses went out to meet his father in-law, bowed down and kissed him. And they asked each other about their well being, and they went into the tent. ⁸ And Moses' told his father in-law all that the LORD had done to Pharaoh and to the Egyptian's for Israel's sake, all the hardship that had come upon them on the way, and how the LORD had delivered them.

⁹ Then Jethro rejoiced for all the good which the LORD had done for Israel, whom He had delivered out of the hand of the Egyptians. ¹⁰ And Jethro said, "Blessed be the LORD, who has delivered you out of the hand of the Egyptians and out of the hand of Pharaoh, and who has delivered the people from under the hand of the Egyptians.

¹¹ Now I know that the LORD is greater than all the gods, for in the very thing in which they behaved proudly, He was about them".

¹² Then Jethro, Moses' father in-law, took a burnt offering and other sacrifices to offer to God. And Aaron came with all the elders of Israel to eat bread with Moses' father in-law before God. ¹³ And so it was, on the next day, that Moses sat to judge the people, and the people stood before Moses from morning until evening.

¹⁴ So when Moses' father in-law saw all that he did for the people, he said, "What is this thing that you are doing for the people? Why do you sit alone, and all the people stand before you from morning until evening"?

¹⁵ And Moses' said to his father in-law, "Because the people come to me to inquire of God. ¹⁶ When they have difficulty they come to me, and I judge between one and another; and I make known the statutes of God and His laws".

¹⁷ So Moses' father in-law said to him, "The thing you do is not good.¹⁸ Both you and these people who are with you will surely wear yourselves out. For this thing is too much for you; you are not able to perform it by yourself.¹⁹ Listen now to my voice, I will give you counsel, and God will be with you. Stand before God for the people, so that you may bring the difficulties to God.²⁰ And you shall teach them the statutes and the

laws, and show them the way in which they must walk and work they must do. ²¹ Moreover you shall select from all the people, able men such as fear God, men of truth, hating covetousness, and place such over them to be rulers of thousands, rulers of hundreds, rulers of fifties, and rulers of tens. ²² And let them judge the people at all times. Then it will be that every matter they shall bring to you, but every small matter they themselves shall judge. So it will be easier for you, for they will bear the burden with you. ²³ If you do this thing, and God so commands you, then you will be able to endure, and all this people will also go to their place of peace". ²⁴ Moses heeded the voice of his father in-law and did all that he had said.

²⁵ And Moses chose able men out of all Israel, and made them heads over the people, rulers of thousands, rulers of hundreds, rulers of fifties, and rulers of tens. ²⁶ So they judged the people at all times; the hard cases they brought to Moses, but they judged every small case themselves. ²⁷ Then Moses let his father in-law depart, and he went his way to his own land.

Who was Jethro?

Jethro was a high Priest. Moses, though called, was made and Jethro was his mentor. When Moses narrated his exploits to Jethro his spiritual father, Jethro made a sacrifice and broke bread. Jethro knew Moses' capacity. Leadership knows capacity and can predict the future; Jethro introduced order and peace in Israel.

Jethro's Principles

1. Jethro's principles discourages the leaders:

    a. From carrying the burden alone.

    b. That feel that their people are not competent.

    c. Who feel that the good ones always run away and incompetent ones stay.

    d. That don't delegate authority; do only that which only you can do.

2. Jethro's principles encourage someone to practice or delegate responsibility.

3. Jethro's principles focus on helping the leader carry the burden.

10 Principles of Jethro

(1) Team work entails doing things with the leader.

(2) Plurality of leadership: a multiplied fraction of your person.

(3) Impartation: receiving the gift of the prophet.

(4) Delegations of authority: this indicates sharing responsibilities and duties.

(5) Unity of control and purpose.

(6) Definition of responsibility- that is, you do not give responsibilities without proper definitions.

(7) Organisation- that is, bringing order.

(8) Focus: to avoid distraction, focus is inevitable and this also indicates concentrating all the efforts in achieving a definite goal.

(9) Accountability.
And over three presidents; of Daniel was first; that the princess might have accounts unto them, and the king should have no damage.[2] This indicates that delegated leaders must be accountable to the people.

(10) Submission to authority: this indicates that all imparted leaders must learn to remain submissive to the anointing. This is something you learn, it is not given by God.

---

[2] Daniel 6:2

Chapter 10

Power to Minister

To be an effective minister of the Gospel, you must be intimate with Christ.[1] There must be a perfect understanding of whom you are serving. Sadly, most ministers don't have a strong intimacy with Christ. Your level of intimacy with Christ in the secret will always show in the open. So to be an effective minister, you must pursue a perfect relationship with Christ.

Intimacy with Christ affects your life and ministry. Most of the time we study, pray and worship but there is no intimacy. The paramount issue is a deep personal walk with Christ; without which these other actions are mere rituals. Many pastors prepare messages to preach from their head. This is a major error. They don't receive revelations from God and as such, they do not go far. You must experience Christ for yourself before you can impart Christ to others. Don't go and plan what to preach because your brain cannot communicate the word of God.

Intimacy with God should precede all ministry activities.

Your fellowship with Christ must be constant for all the years of your life in ministry. You need that fellowship to remain relevant.

Delivering Your Message

A servant will not be corrected by words, for though he understands he will not answer.[2]

---
[1] Mark 3:13-14
[2] Proverbs 29:19

Topic-Title-Objective

In message delivery, it is not every word you speak that makes impact, but every word of God given must make impact. To achieve this, you must do the following:

(a) Ask God to give you a definite objective. The objective the Holy Spirit has given you is what you deliver. An effective message is one which produces the desired and expected end or results.

(b) In your message delivery, always asses yourself with long-term results (a period of 1 year at least).

(c) When you know what God has to say, you must be able to summarise it in a visionary statement which gives you a topic or title of your message.

Subject

I will hear what the Lord God will speak, for he will speak peace unto his people, and to his saints, but let them not turn again to folly.[3]

I will stand upon my watch; and set me upon the tower, and will watch to see what he will say unto me, what I shall answer when I am reproved.[4]

You must have a perfect understanding of your God-given subject and analyse the message so as to:

(a) Minister to people

(b) And to yourself because a God-given message does not only minister to the crowd. It also ministers to you.

Audience

But now brethren, if I come to you speaking with tongues, what shall I profit you unless I speak to you either by revelation, by knowledge or by prophesying, or by teaching. Even things without life, whether flute

---
[3] Psalms 85:8
[4] Habakkuk 2:1

or harp, when they make a sound, unless they make a distinction in the sounds, how will it be known, what is piped or played? For if the trumpet makes an uncertain sound, who will prepare for battle? So likewise you, unless you utter by the tongue words easy to understand, how will it be known what is spoken? For ye shall speak into the air. There are, it may be, so many kinds of languages in the world, and none of them is without significance. Therefore, I do not know the meaning of the language, I shall be a foreigner to him who speaks, and he who speaks will be a foreigner to me.*[5]*

You must know your audience and understand how the spirit wants you to communicate effectively. You must consciously study and understand.

(a) The educational background of the people

(b) The spiritual background of the people

(c) The financial background of the people

(d) The expository background (exposure) of the people

(e) The mentality of the people

It is the knowledge of your audience that determines the language of communication. You must have a perfect understanding of the people. As you teach, you study the response or reaction of the people.

Communication

To communicate effectively, your presentation must be properly organized.

Parts of a Message

Every effective message is composed of at least 3 main parts:

(a) Introduction

(b) Main body

---

[5] 1 Corinthians 14:6-11

(c) Conclusion

An effective message must have the advantage of a strong introduction. Your introduction has to be strong. Also, you have got to have a powerful main body and a smashing conclusion.

A delivery is likely to be a flop if it doesn't have any of these parts.

After hearing from God, develop a vision and address the people's minds to focus on the message. This is because the beginning of a message, definitely, determines the flow of the message. Your statement must be presented in a way to:

(d) Arrest wandering minds.

(e) Connect yourself to your audience.

(f) Set the tempo and the directions of the message.

(g) Create a desire in people's hearts to receive what you have to offer.

index

3 Effective Methods of Soul Winning 17
5-fold ministry
   the gift of Jesus 66
5 leadership levels 14
6 Facts About Soulwinning 33

A

Abraham 33, 41, 42, 65
ambassadors for Christ 66
anointed brain, planning 17
authority of God 72

B

Believers 16, 77
boldness
   7 preaching qualities 25

C

Christendom 15, 33
Christians 68, 69, 75
church, authority 45
Church, Christ's love 16
church system 32
clear conscience 68

D

David 29, 44, 71, 83
delegations 86
dieting 24
diligence 31
disciple 32
discipline and character 18
divine contact 26

divine direction 44
divine nature 20

E

effective preacher 27, 28
Eleazer's principles
   12 things regarding a faithful steward 40
Elijah 46
Elisha 46
Enthusiasm 18
eternal life 68, 75
eternal life, gift of 14
evangelism 15
Evangelism 18
evangelist, work of 70
everlasting life 24

F

faithfulness 33
familiarity, danger of 20
fasting, praying 47
fervency 57
fight of faith 68, 75

G

gift of God 21, 79
gifts, development of 29
glory of God 29
goal-oriented 20
godly nature 28
godly relationships 69
good conscience 68, 74
good doctrine 21
good soldier

INDEX

ministry, suffering 74
Gospel 16, 73, 74, 75, 87
Gospel, minister of 15
Gospel, preaching 27

H

hard work
  7 preaching qualities 31, 58
hard work, consistent 58
health, tongue of the wise 27
healthy body 24
healthy living 24
healthy spirit 24
Holy Spirit 38, 76, 80, 88

I

imagination
  7 preaching qualities 26
imagination, power of 26
immorality, sexual desires 36
individual ideology 77
intercessions 69
intimate with Christ
  effective ministry 87

J

Jacob 29, 42, 65
Jesus Christ 67, 74
Jethro 83, 85, 86
Judas 46

K

knowledge of the truth 23

L

leadership authorities, submission 45
leadership, capacity building 40
leadership, growth and success 21
love 42, 43, 54, 67, 68, 72, 76, 78, 79

M

mentorship
  spiritual authority 67
message, planning 30
minister's attire 20
ministerial demands 75
ministerial limelight 17
ministerial performance 21
ministerial skills 26
ministry, balanced 77
ministry, Christian responsibility 74
ministry, dressing 81
ministry, essential tools
  spiritual gifts 73
ministry, good administration 77
ministry, maturity in 27
ministry, organization
  order, leadership institution 76
ministry, standard 73
ministry, team work 86
ministry, warfare 75
Moses 83, 85

O

obedience to God's will 14
offering, prophet's 62
offering, thanksgiving 62
One God 23
openness, quality of 14
ordination into ministry 23

P

parables 26
Pastor 20, 29, 30, 66, 68, 72, 75, 77, 81
patience 37, 64, 68, 72, 78
Paul 80
physical appearance and dressing
  7 preaching qualities 24
physical fitness

INDEX

7 preaching qualities 19
planning 51
planning, components
  sound plan 51
planning, corporate
  types of planning 51
planning, general
  types of planning 51
planning, personal
  types of planning 29
prayer and fasting 74
prayers 30, 69
prayer, time with God 28
preparation, planning 27
priesthood 36
production 59
pure heart 68, 78

R

reality of Christ 18
regular ministers 20
religion 37
reproduction
  5 leadership levels 20
rest 24
role model
  leadership 29, 72, 73

S

sacred desk 26, 27
salvation, God's plan of 18
salvation, source of 18
satanic attacks
  ministry, warfare 75
satanic traps 18
Saul 71, 83
scriptures, studying 26
searching for God, 26
self confidence 37
sense of imagination 57
sincere faith 68

soul winning 28
  a guarantee for eternal honour and glory 29
  love is the key 26
soul-winnning, expression of wisdom 20
Spirit of God 32
Spirit of Jesus 32
spiritual authority 71
spiritual forces
  ministry, warfare 75
spiritual territories 30
stewards, deceitful 34
stewards, faithful 38
supplications 69

T

teaching skills 17
testimony, effective, personal 18
the Word of God, double-edged sword 17
the Word, washing of water 16
tithing 62
tongue of the wise 27

U

unbelievers 16

W

walking with God, Enoch 44
wisdom problems
  lack of wisdom 56
wisdom, prosperity
  ministry and finance 56
wise in heart 17
witnessing 21
Word of truth 18
word of truth, rightly dividing 21
word of truth, sharing 21

About the Author

Pastor Love Judah, and his wife, Shallom Judah are the founding pastors of Love Judah Ministries International, a 5-faceted ministry:

Truth Assembly International Churches
Crystal Vessels International
Women on Fire Campaign
Love Media International
Love Missions International.

They are blessed with four children and live in Owerri, Imo State, Nigeria.

www.ingramcontent.com/pod-product-compliance
Lightning Source LLC
Chambersburg PA
CBHW030054170426
43197CB00010B/1523